The Treasure of the Silver Web

The Treasure of the Silver Web

Marian Green

Thoth Publications
Loughborough Leicestershire

A CIP catalogue record for this book is available from the British Library.

Printed and bound in Great Britain

Published by Thoth Publications
64, Leopold Street, Loughborough, LE11 5DN

ISBN 978-1-870450-77-5
Web address www.thoth.co.uk
email: enquiries@thoth.co.uk

This book is dedicated to the Real Paul and his family, the real Clover and the really mystical realm of Dartmoor.

Introduction

Once upon a time.... for that is how many adventure stories began when I was a young girl (and many people would say I am an old lady now) some people were brought together by fate and had magical adventures...

Chapter One
An Accidental Meeting

With a wild yell, Paul, missing his grip on a branch above his head, half slid, half tumbled through the hedge to land on his knees, with a soft bump. A black and white mongrel bounded up to him, snuffled his face as he struggled to his feet and gave his ear a damp lick as he stood up out of reach. Looking around him Paul discovered a woman standing a bit further along the hedge through which he had just fallen. She had fairly long dark hair pulled back into a pony tail, dark sparkling eyes and a wide grin on her face as she moved towards Paul.

'Are you all right?' she asked, putting down her basket which was half filled with shiny black berries, 'You did come through that hedge with a bit of a wallop.'

'I'm ok,' replied Paul cautiously, 'is this your field?'

'Yes, I live in that cottage there,' the woman pointed to a steep thatched roof that loomed over a tangled growth of trees and bushes edging the meadow.

Paul examined her, she was wearing faded jeans and a shirt which had seen better days but there was something about her that many grown-ups didn't have. She had not shouted at him for crashing into her field, she hadn't even seemed particularly surprised that a lad should be clambering about in the hedge.

'Aren't those berries poisonous?' Paul asked, having been warned that anything not bought in shops was certain to be deadly in the country.

'No, they are elderberries, I use them for wine or jam,' the woman answered, 'hey, you seem to have cut your arm, look.'

Paul glanced at his sleeve and saw that it had a long tear and the skin underneath showed a jagged scratch from which blood oozed, staining the blue cloth in a dramatic manner.

'It's ok,' he said, just becoming aware of the sharp stinging pain. He bent down to pick up the branches which he had gathered and which had been the reason he had been in the hedge in the first place.

'I'll give it a wash when I get home, Mum can look at it tonight when she gets back if it is mucky.' He turned to walk towards the gate in the hedge leading back to the lane from which he had clambered up the banking.

'What are those branches for? It's a bit early for Harvest Festival decorations for the church.' the woman asked, without sounding nosey.

'Biology project at school,' Paul muttered, 'we have to get as many sorts of specimens of trees and shrubs from a local hedge as we can and the teacher is going to tell us how old that bit of hedge is. There is a formula to work it out with. I got this lot between the gate and the place where I fell through. I was reaching for that tree there,' he pointed upwards, 'the one with pleated leaves, to add to the collection.'

'That's a hornbeam,' the woman replied, 'one of the hardest woods in Britain, hence the name.'

'Come off it,' Paul laughed, 'there's no such thing as hornbeam…'

'Ask your teacher then,' said the woman, looking around for her dog, 'but it is a real tree. That one there is hawthorn, another is ash,' she said pointing to the wilting specimens in his hand, 'do you know all the names?'

'No, I'll have to look them up at school, I bet the others know what these things are,' he muttered, 'where I come from all the trees are the same, big leafy things with scabby trunks that peel off and are yellow underneath. Nothing else grows in Hoxton.'

'Those trees are London planes, pretty well adapted to the polluted air in cities. There are lots of them in Paris, too, and other smoky places. When do you have to finish the project?'

'We're supposed to hand it all in next Monday but unless I can find some information at home I will have to wait till I get into the school library on Monday and so be late. My Dad knows as much about trees as I do about his rotten plastics so he won't help, and Mum is always busy cooking something or washing or yelling for us to find things. No, I'll have to wait till Monday and old Larky will be mad.'

'I have several books on trees. If it would be of any help you are welcome to have a look at them. If you have time that is.' The woman patted her dog's head as it stretched up her with hairy white paws.

'Well,' said Paul, gazing at the thatched roof buried in its sea of greenery, 'I need to be back by six as Mum and Dad get in from their daily grind then. What's the time now?'

The woman glanced at her watch, 'Ten to four, just about time for a cup of tea.'

Paul glanced back towards the roofs of the village which had so recently become his home and remembered what his father had said when they were about to quit London, 'At least in the country there is less mugging and street crime. People have been there for generations and it takes years to be accepted but it is safe to be out at night. Paul will probably make friends with the local kids and we will get to know their parents. It will be ok after a while, once we settle into the rural life. I expect the villagers will talk to us after a bit...'

'Oh, all right, but I'd better not be late. What's your dog called?'

'Clover, look at her back view,' Paul watched the dog as she scampered across the field, her white body almost dazzling against the green grass, but she had a black face and on her bottom there was a clear clover leaf design of black fur with her tail making the stalk, half black and half white.

'Her mother was a Welsh collie but we don't know about her father,' said the woman, smiling, 'she is four and very intelligent. Here, Clover.' The dog ran back to her mistress, black face split by a wide doggy grin, her pink tongue lolling over sharp white teeth. She bounded to Paul's side and nudged his hand with a chilly black nose.

'She likes you and that is a good sign. I always distrust folk who are not liked by dogs or cats or young children,' she said, 'come on then, did you gather all your twigs for your collection?'

'Yes, they're all here, for what it's worth.' Paul replied and, without knowing quite why, picked up the basket of elder-berries and followed the woman towards her cottage.

There was a narrow wooden gate set deep in the shaggy hedge which made a boundary to her garden and beyond it a winding path, paved with brown local stone, leading to a green door set into a stone porch. On the left of the path were strange green plants but to the right, leading towards the front of the cottage, were great banks of coloured flowers of every type and description. Paul could recognise roses, of course, and tall hollyhocks, chrysanthemums and michaelmas daisies but the rest of the flowers and plants were beyond his power to put a name to. Before he had time to more than guess what some of them were he found himself being ushered into the porch. Like most country houses it was crammed with wellington boots, macintoshes, walking sticks and all manner of grubby items which were too dirty to bring into the house.

As the cottage had a rather low-browed aspect, its thatch seeming to reach almost to the ground, he had expected it to be dim and spooky inside as cottages in TV plays tended to be, but he was surprised. The porch led into the kitchen which did have a low ceiling and dark shelves on some of the walls but along the length of the side above the sink was a wide, modern double glazed window looking out onto the vegetable garden behind the cottage. The walls and ceiling, where they weren't hidden by shelves laden with jars and pots and bottles of country goodies, were white and the floor was cool, grey stone. In a recess was a large cream Aga cooker and on one of its closed lids a big black kettle stood, steam gently rising from its spout. Paul looked around in fascination. He had often seen films of cottages but this was the first time he had ever been inside one. From the bright rag rugs on the floor to the serried ranks of jars on the shelves filled with red and green and purple fruits or preserves climbing up to the beams above it seemed like a cave of wonders.

'Tea or coffee?' his hostess asked, 'or would you like a glass of fruit juice? I have apple and plum juice in the fridge.'

'Coffee, please, if you don't mind,' Paul replied, jerking his attention back to reality, 'Mum and Dad are always drinking tea but I like coffee best.'

'As we are English,' the woman said, 'I suppose we ought to introduce ourselves. I am Diana Dymond, what is your name?'

'I'm Paul Sparrow,' he answered, and waited for the joke or pun that his name usually brought.

'That is nice,' Diana said, 'there are lots of folk round here named after birds or plants like Raven or Ashwood. The grocer is Mr Butterwort and there is Dr Martin whose surgery is at Swallow House. Many old surnames were chosen from natural things or trades, like Baker or Cook or Mason. My family have been here in this cottage for about 400 years and there have always been Dymonds in the West Country since time out of mind.'

Diana took two brightly painted mugs from hooks on the dresser and a jar of instant coffee from the beam above the Aga, then lifting the great black kettle from the stove made coffee for them both. She fetched a bottle of milk from a large fridge and then took down a round cake tin from one of the shelves. For a moment she struggled to get the lid off then handed the tin to Paul. 'Open that if you can. Do you take sugar? I only use brown because it tastes better,' she said reaching yet another pottery jar from the shelf.

'One and a half, please' Paul answered, and after a short wrench and twist he got the lid off the tin. Inside were flat, crumbly-looking brown biscuity things. Diana reached inside and put a handful onto a plate. Clover nudged her mistress's leg, wagging her tail frantically and smiling her doggy best, drooling for a taste of human biscuit.

'Say please then,' and the dog sat on her tail, paws raised and a pleading look in her intelligent brown eyes. Diana gave her a small piece and looked down again 'was that nice then?' Clover licked her lips then lay down, her head between her paws, 'woof' she barked gently.

'Come on Paul, let's go into the other room where we can sit down. That's your coffee in the red mug, bring the flapjacks and I'll fend off this starving beast.'

She crossed the kitchen, passed through a dimly lit hall from which a twisting staircase led upwards and entered another brightly lit room. Across the whole of the back wall were double glazed windows and a metal framed door gave onto a lawn surrounded by more flowers with vegetables standing in neat rows to the left. Diana waved Paul into a chair by the deep fireplace. It was not cold enough to light the great pile of logs that lay there ready, mixed with pine cones and crumpled coloured paper for effect. A huge beam spanned the wide hearth and in a diamond shape cut into the wood was an ornate letter 'D'.

Paul was delighted by this strange place and could hardly cease from staring about him. The walls of this room were lined with shelves too, but in place of the jams and pickles here were books, a whole library full Paul thought. Among the books were stones, carvings and statues, models of birds and animals, a positive treasure house of interesting things. Later on, Paul described the room as a cross between a bookshop and a museum yet it was also lived in. Diana offered Paul the flapjacks and he found them sweet and crunchy, discovering they had nuts and other good things in. Clover lay before him doing her starving dog act, trying to pretend she hadn't been fed for days. After his second biscuit Paul gave in and offered her a small corner. She took it delicately with her black lips. 'Was that nice then?' he asked and Clover licked her lips and then his hand.

'Daft dog,' Diana said, 'leave him alone, we have work to do.'

She reached up the bookshelves and selected a large volume. Beckoning Paul she went to an old table near the window and opened the book. On one page was a picture of a tree with a close up of leaves, flowers and fruits and on the other closely written words. Here and there, underlined or printed in italics to show a foreign language, was a description of the tree. It was open at Ash. Paul realised that he had left his bundle of twigs in the kitchen and went quickly to fetch them. The leaves looked a bit wilted but he hoped they would be sufficiently alive to match the pictures. When he returned Diana had placed a pen and a pad of lined paper by the book so that Paul could copy down any information he needed for his project.

'Do the big trees first then go onto the shrubs. I know what most of them are so you do the research and I will help if you get stuck, otherwise your teacher might think you have cheated if you come from London and are now familiar with different varieties of trees.'

Diana turned away, picking up another book from a pile beside a chair and slumped into its deep cushions.

'Ash – Common Ash, Fraxinus excelsior, leaves long, lanceolate, odd-pinnage, 3-6 pairs...' at first Paul didn't understand then it dawned on him that it meant the shape and arrangement, although the bit about the flowers being borne in pannicles and the fruit being slightly twisted samara with ellipsiod seeds was confusing. Anyway, he copied out the details that were clear and then turned over the pages seeking his other specimens. After naming most of the samples he was turning through the book when, much to his astonishment, he came upon 'Hornbeam, common, Carpinus betulus with oblong, pointed leaves, doubly serrate margins and all, and a picture of the tree he had been reaching for when he fell through the hedge. Its wood was described as heavy and hard just as Diana Dymond had said. He identified hawthorn, blackthorn, ash, hazel, honeysuckle, twiny stuff called travellers' joy or old man's beard, brambles, which he knew about, especially the sharp thorns which had torn his shirt, wild or dog rose, another prickly plant and poisonous woody nightshade. Paul finished copying bits of information about each plant and walked over to Diana to see what she was doing. She was immersed in a large picture book of cookery, 'That looks tasty,' said Paul, pointing to a colourful plate of roast chicken, surrounded by bright green and orange vegetables. Diana, following his pointing finger again noticed the deep scratch along his arm and put down her book immediately.

'You had better clean that scratch up before you go home or your mother will think you have been in a fight. Go to the kitchen and wash it, there is plenty of hot water in the tap, and I will get a pot of something to help it heal.'

Without another word she rose to her feet and vanished through another door off the hall. Paul went to the kitchen and ran the taps over the stainless steel sink. The water was scalding hot but he added some cold through the mixer and, rolling up his sleeve, or what was left of it, examined his wound. There was a crooked line running from his elbow to the back of his left hand, dark with dried blood, and something black and hard on the back of his hand. He rinsed the cut, watching the stream of water turn pink, but on the back of his hand he found a thorn stuck in his skin. He couldn't get a grasp of it with either his fingers or his teeth but just then Diana returned carrying a small white jar with a black lid.

'Has it come clean?' she asked, reaching for a clean towel from the rack over the Aga.

'Yes, it's ok, but there is a prickle stuck in my hand, I'll have to get Mum's tweezers to pull it out.'

Diana opened a drawer in the dresser, rummaged for a moment then presented him with a shiny pair of pointed tweezers. 'I use those for pulling out rose thorns when I'm gardening. Can you manage or would you like me to try?'

Paul hated being mothered and picking up the offered instrument caught the end of the thorn and pulled in out. He was biting his lip a bit as he pulled and a drop of red blood oozed out and trickled across his hand, but it was out in one piece.

'I've done it,' he said, returning to the sink to rinse the place.

Diana handed him the towel and he dabbed his arm dry. Most of the scratch was just a thin red mark but the back of his hand looked a bit puffy and was still bleeding. Picking up the pot from the table, Diana said 'Put a bit of this on, it will take away the sting and stop it going septic or anything.'

Instead of the usual blue tube of ointment his mother used she gave Paul a pottery jar with no label except a hand written one saying "OINTMENT" in old fashioned letters. He unscrewed the lid and instead of smooth white cream there was a dark green jelly which smelled strongly of country things.

'What is it?' he asked sharply, 'I don't want witches' potions. I'll be all right.'

'It is a local balm made from plants rather than chemicals like the stuff you buy in the chemists. It is quite safe with thyme and comfrey. Even toothpastes and mouthwashes have thymol in, that is extracted from thyme, and comfrey is that big green plant by the path.' She pointed out of the window, 'it won't sting or anything and I assure you it is quite safe.'

Paul hesitated but the smell was pleasant and he dipped a finger tip into the jelly. It felt cool and clean so he gently smeared a bit on the elbow end of the scratch. The stuff didn't sting like some things his mother used and it vanished into his skin without a sticky mess. Carefully his spread the balm along the cut even on the deep bit on the back of his hand. It seemed to feel better already.

'Hey, that's good, it doesn't hurt and it feels...'

'Yes, it is meant to, it is made of living plant juices not dead chemicals so it ought to work better.' Diana took away the jar and walked out through the door, Paul followed, drawn by curiosity. There was a door under the stairs that he hadn't noticed. Inside was a dim room with an aromatic smell, a bit like some posh aftershave someone had given his Dad one Christmas, spicy and sweet and very strange. Beside the door stood a besom, a garden broom, propped in a corner and there were all sorts of jars and THINGS, shapes and shadows that he couldn't make out in the dim light. Diana replaced the jar and came back to him. She was smiling, but not in a sinister way, friendly and amused, as if he had told her a joke but he hadn't said a word.

'Come on then,' she said, 'there is just time to have a look at the garden, then you ought to go home. It is nearly half past five.'

Paul returned to the book-filled room and gathered his shrivelling samples and the pages of notes he had made then followed Diana back through the kitchen and the cluttered porch into the side garden.

'Why are all those things green and those over there ordinary flowers?' Paul asked, unaware that most of his conversation had been questions.

'These green plants are mostly herbs, mint for sauce to eat with lamb, sage for sage and bacon pudding, parsley for salads. Those thin ones are chives, you may have seen cream cheese with chives in the supermarket. That is thyme, used in the ointment, smell it.' She bent down and picked a sprig of small darkish leaves and crushed them between her fingers. Paul sniffed the sweetish scent which reminded him of Italian restaurants in London.

'These herbs are for healing. Comfrey which is also called boneset because you can make a sort of plaster of its leaves, valerian, greater celandine, tansy, camomile, which makes a pleasant tea. There are heaps more but I'll tell you about them some other time if you are interested. Have you got all your papers and tree branches? Come out through the front gate. I expect you know that no-one uses front doors in the country except strangers or for weddings and funerals. Anyway, here is the lane back to the village.'

She was just about to turn back into her cottage when she called 'Do you like mushrooms? There are a lot in the field next to this one and I hope to pick some tomorrow morning, early. If your mother would like some they have a lot more flavour than shop ones and these are free for the gathering. If you would like to come be here about eight with a basket and we will see what we can find. Cheerio.'

Without waiting for an answer she turned back into the house, slapping her thigh to call Clover who was chasing something invisible along the foot of the hedge.

'What a strange person,' thought Paul as he jogged back home, 'not like a grown up at all, and what a strange cottage too, all ancient and modern rolled into one. Why does she have all those books and what is that dark room for with the broomstick and herbs and that?' An odd dog too, clever and not pushy. I do like mushrooms and bacon and Mum does a super thing with chicken and mushrooms, just like Chinese takeaway...'

When he got home and began to explain his afternoon's activities his parents were hardly listening. His mother was cooking a stew and his Dad was buried in a pile of trade magazines on scintillating plastic. His mother said she would like some mushrooms so long as they were the right sort and his Dad was pleased he had met one of the local girls and got on good terms with her, 'and don't pick red toadstools...'

When he went to bed he examined his arm and found that most of it was fading to a pinkish line with a darker bit where the thorn had been. 'Call me early even though it is Saturday,' he shouted down the stairs, 'I want to get some of those mushrooms before the cows eat them or whatever makes them disappear later on.'

Chapter Two
Wild Harvesting

'Paul, are you getting up? It's half past seven. Can you get some lunch if your Dad and I go shopping in Exeter? We want all sorts of things which these village shops just don't stock. There is a cold chicken in the fridge and some salad or else a tin of soup or something on toast. You won't go bothering your Mrs Dymond, will you? And put a clean shirt on….' his mother's voice faded as she bustled about the little house. Paul struggled up and peered out of his bedroom window. He hadn't yet really got used to seeing so much sky. Beyond the roof of the cottage opposite there was a vast clear blue sweep, paling towards the distant horizon where the misty purple-blue moors rose up to meet it; very different from the terrace across the street where he had lived before. All you could see from there was a tower block of council flats and the chimneys of a factory down by the canal. Often the sky in London looked dim but here it was misty blue and streaked with pinkish clouds.

Clumping downstairs after a lick and a promise of a wash in the bathroom, Paul went into the kitchen. Here the colours were yellow and cream with orange drawers and tablecloth instead of gloomy grey and off-white like the Hoxton house. Sunlight streamed in through the window filtered through some trails of rose stems laden with scented yellow blossoms which scrambled all over the sides of the house. Quickly Paul downed a cup of tea and scrunched through a bowl of cornflakes with hardly any milk as the bottle was empty and the milkman didn't call in this rural, cow infested place until nearly lunchtime.

'I'll be ok, I can find something to eat or go to Ye Olde Tea Shope in Hill Street if you leave me some money.'

'You can't have scones and jam and clotted cream for lunch,' said his father, wiping oily hands on a piece of kitchen towel after tinkering with his car engine, 'surely you can manage to prepare something to eat out of the freezer.'

'Don't worry, Dad, if I get those mushrooms I am off after I can fry them with bread and bacon and a couple of eggs and tomatoes and anything else I can find. I don't intend to starve.'

'Don't you go ruining my new cooker either my lad, no eating anything you're not certain about. You better wait till I get in to look at your mushrooms and anything else you pick, goodness knows what you might eat. I don't want to come back and find you lying poisoned in my nice clean kitchen.' his mother scolded but patted him on the shoulder as he slid out of the kitchen door.

'See ya.' he called, jogging down the lane with a plastic box which had once held ice cream in the freezer, in case he did get any mushrooms.

It was ten past eight when he went through the gate from the field into the side of Diana Dymond's garden. He was just about to knock on the porch door when there was a great flurry and rattle of claws on the stone floor within and a volley of barks as Clover announced his arrival to her mistress.

'Down, daft dog,' shouted Diana over the barking and scrabbling which sounded as it they were having a battle to reach the door first. Paul stepped back as it was flung open and Clover, closely followed by Diana, rushed into the garden.

'I will just get a jacket and a basket for our finds and some plastic bags in case there are any sloes in the hedge in the bottom field.'

Within moments she was back, today wearing green and carrying an anorak which had faded to a dull khaki colour. Clover bounded around both of them, showing excitement far greater than a foraging party ought to have evoked, but her mistress firmly closed the garden gate, shutting her in. They crossed the field where they had met the day before and climbed over a gate into the next field.

'Always go over the hinge end if you have to climb a gate,' Diana said, passing over the basket and box to Paul. 'Don't scare any cattle or sheep in a field and leave the gate as you find it. People often think you should always close gates but if a farmer has opened it to drive a tractor through or a herd of animals it is no joke finding it shut.'

'Are there bulls?' asked Paul as he caught sight of a herd of black cattle on the far side of the field.

'No, bulls are usually kept on their own, they always have a ring through their noses and unless you frighten them will not run at you. Those are beef cattle and you will see they back away as you get near. Cows for milk will often come and inspect you if you cross their pasture but they are more likely to walk away than come at you.'

The cattle, as predicted, moved away, even the ones lying down chewing the cut rose to their feet in the awkward way cattle have and moved off backwards. Soon they had crossed to the far hedge and Diana began to inspect the ground. The grass was dew wet and soon soaked the hems of their jeans and Paul's trainers. Diana was wearing muddy wellingtons, obviously more prepared on her home ground.

'They used to keep horses in this field and the next and often you find mushrooms there but we don't seem to be lucky here today. Let us go through the next field and see what turns up. There are sheep there.' Before she could unravel the bit of binder twine which held the next gate shut a black and white bombshell burst through the staring cattle and bounded over to Diana, jumping up to lick her face.

'Get down, Clover, you mutt, I thought you were shut in. Sit!' she yelled as her dog danced gaily round her. Clover sank to the ground, her ears drooping beside her black face, her bushy tail beating the ground in a half-hearted manner.

'Now you behave yourself and stay to heel or I will tie you up. If you scare those sheep or even start playing games with them, rounding them up like your mother, I will take you home.'

The dog seemed to understand every word and crept close to her mistress's heels as they entered the gate and walked across the closely nibbled grass. Suddenly Diana spotted a whitish dome in the grass and stooped to pick it. She held the mushroom out to Paul.

'Smell that, it is a field mushroom, a bit bigger than the sort you get in plastic boxes at Sainsburys I expect. Look, you can tell it is the right sort by peeling an edge. Proper mushrooms peel cleanly, other fungi that look like them don't, nor do they smell right. These are so good you can eat them raw or chopped up in salads. They usually seem to grow in clusters, look, in that longer clump of grass there are several.'

Soon they were both stooping and picking the firm white mushrooms, some were open and flatter with dark brown gills underneath, others were tightly curled with only a tiny bit of pinkish gills showing beneath their caps. Paul found a huge flat mushroom, wider than his hand.

'That is a horse mushroom but they are nice to eat so long as there aren't any little weevils in it.' Diana told him, examining it with an expert eye.

Suddenly Paul spotted what looked like a golf ball, he picked it thinking it to be a small closed mushroom but it was rounder and had slight marks on its top.

'That is a puffball, don't throw it away. They are very good to eat too. They are solid inside and can be sliced and fried with bacon just like field mushrooms. There is a kind called the giant puffball which grows up to a foot across but you don't often see them round here. Make sure those are not soft or they are too ripe and will burst into dark grey spores like powder.'

Paul was soon good at recognising mushrooms and puffballs and between them they had a fair collection. Diana had gradually worked her way through the field towards the far hedge, Clover at her heels. The dog had given a preliminary sniff at the mushrooms and then tried to wander off on her own business but Diana called her sharply to heel and she lay down, black head on white paws, and only moved when here mistress went on, though her eyes followed the sheep which browsed on the rich autumnal grass.

When they had picked all the available mushrooms and inspected the hedge where Diana was disappointed to find there were no sloes worth picking, nor anything else they could fill their bags with, they set off back towards her cottage.

'How is your arm?' she asked as Paul lugged the basket over the far gate.

'It's fine now, there is hardly a mark except where the thorn was. Quite a potion that. You ought to sell it in town. Have you got any more country recipes for curing things?'

'Plenty. I grow dozens of herbs and most of them have several uses, and there are lots of other wild or semi-cultivated fruits and berries which can be used for wine and jam, for pickles and in salads if you know what you are about. There are also other things, stones and wells with strange powers, according to local legends,' Diana waved her free hand towards the circling moors. 'This part of the country has been inhabited since the first people came to Britain, and up on the moors there are still the walls of their houses standing after four or five thousand years. They put up standing stones to mark special places, they made rings and mounts with pointers which show where the sun or moon or some of the stars will rise at special dates of the year. They even made notches on the skyline so that travellers could see the road even if the hills were miles away.'

'Go on,' said Paul, as they wandered back towards the gate, 'no-one was civilised until the Romans came, the people here wore woad and were barbarians. Romans built roads and towns and things like that according to our history lessons.'

Diana laughed 'Certainly the Romans built towns and paved roads and designed many fine things but the ancient people of Britain built great earthworks requiring as much effort as a motorway, they put up circles of standing stones like Stonehenge so accurately that the sun still rises exactly through the correct slot like a coin going into a fruit machine. Those great stones and many other earthworks were ancient monuments before the Romans even landed here. Our own people knew about stones and wells, crediting them with strange powers and magical qualities, because they had no technical words to use. They named them Gods and Goddesses and told stories to their children about great heroes and their deeds.'

'Like Robin Hood and King Arthur?' Paul queried, 'I have seen some series on TV about them. They never said they were the people who built Stonehenge...' he had now reached the gate.

'Well, not quite,' Diana broke in, 'both King Arthur and Robin Hood were real people but the stories they are best known for are a mixture of real history and older myths, that is traditional tales. Most people think of King Arthur as a knight in shining armour but the historical Arthur lived in the 6th century when they still wore chain mail and place armour, the horses they rode were hardly bigger than what we call ponies now. Not really like Camelot in the film but it is based on facts.'

'What about Merlin then, and all those witches and wizards, I bet their magic wasn't real. Turning people into animals, disappearing and coming alive again. What about that?' Paul challenged.

Diana replied, again looking towards the high hills, 'Well there are stories about the Druids, the old priests who were here before the Christian church was introduced, who were credited with all sorts of strange powers. They were supposed to be able to control the weather, they seemed to be able to call up fogs in which they could hide, whole armies could vanish in moments and then lurk in woods and bushes until their enemies gave up. At other times they could whistle up winds to blow ships with sails out to sea. You can't row a big boat against the wind and tide, you know. Perhaps they have a way of making it rain or thunder, legends tell of such things and we can't be sure. I have seen some very strange things, I must admit.'

Paul looked at her closely. She was a strange person, he felt so – well – at home with her, as if she had been a friend for years, yet they had only met yesterday. She must be quite old but it didn't seem to matter, and now she was telling tales of marvels as if they were as real as the news on TV. She knew all about plants, suggested he could eat toadstools and poison berries for he was still not certain about those elder-berries she had been picking the day before. Maybe everyone in the country was like that, steeped in legends and weird lore of trees and fungi. He had only been in the country six weeks which was not really long enough to know.

He was still thinking about this strange person when they arrived back at the gate of her cottage.

'What about a cup of tea, or coffee if you prefer, or a cold drink as it is so warm for the time of year?' Diana asked as they reached the porch door of the cottage.

'Err-yes,' said Paul, his mind still bemused by what they had been talking about, 'what's your apple juice like?'

'Try it,' Diana went to the big fridge and brought out a tall jug. Taking a glass from a shelf she poured cloudy, pale liquid into it and gave it to Paul. Cautiously he sipped it, not fizzy nor sour, but he thought, tasting of apples, sweet and pleasant.

'Yes, it's nice, better than cheap orange squash, I can't bear that, nor some sorts of blackcurrant juice that we sometimes have in the winter, hot. They taste all metallic and horrid. Did you make that wine with those elder-berries yet?'

'You are always asking questions aren't you,' said Diana, making some coffee with boiling water from the black kettle, 'how about telling me about yourself then I can ask you some in turn. Fair's fair.'

'All right,' he said, 'but it isn't very exciting. I lived in Hoxton in a little terraced house near the Regent's Park Canal and went to school in the next street, then Dad's firm, Apollo Plastics, merged with another that makes special shapes and things and both were offered a new factory down here, on the big new trading estate by the main road. Dad designs special moulds and they wanted him to come down here. Mum is a typist – pardon me – secretary, and got a job with a firm of accountants in Micklehampton very luckily. I go to Daniel Whiddon Comprehensive, up by the swimming pool. We live at Rose Cottage in that estate up behind the Green Man Pub, third one along with yellow roses all over the front. That's about it.'

'Not bad for a brief biography, I would say. What do you want to do?'

'I don't know yet, I quite fancy being an airline pilot but you need lots of A levels for that. I'll have to see how I feel later on. Stuck down here perhaps I could learn to be a naturalist, like on TV and go catching rare animals in steaming jungles, or up unexplored mountains or something... Do you write books or what?' he said, pointing towards the other room, 'or have your own museum?'

'Not books, just reviews for various magazines; brief accounts of what the book is about and if it is interesting. Mostly cookery or country life and herbs, of course. My museum, as you call it, are things gathered when I used to travel as a writer for a women's journal, but I got fed up with roaming the world, living out of a suitcase and longed to come home here where my family have lived for over 400 years,' she paused, sipping her coffee, 'I had not been back long when both my parents were killed when their car crashed off the road on the moor, in deep snow, so I inherited Rowans –

this cottage. Now I write a bit, garden more, and if people come to me with problems or needing medicines I can often help them with herbal balms or teas or other traditional remedies. It is very quiet and I got to like people when I worked in cities, so now I talk to anyone who comes my way. Even the dullest-seeming individual may have some interesting tale to tell or experience to relate. I also like to share my wild harvesting, if anyone is interested. Most folk prefer the things they can get in packets or tins from Mr Butterwort, which is a shame, because there are many wild fruits and plants there for the effort of picking,' Diana sighed

'You were talking earlier about heroes and magic and potions. Do you really believe that sort of thing nowadays? I don't see how witches could fly through the air on broomsticks, or wizards turn people into frogs – that must be a load of nonsense.' Paul goaded.

'Well, it depends on what you understand by 'magic'. If you come to think of it, hearing music and seeing pictures out of thin air would have been thought of as magic, and flying through the air was the work of demons, but now we have television and aircraft,' Diana replied, mildly.

'Yes, but that's different, that's technology not magic,' said Paul, frowning, 'you still can't explain, well... magic.'

'It is an art of causing changes, making things happen which seemed unlikely at the beginning, balancing things in this world of TV and science with another world where magical powers work. It isn't easy to explain because words change what you are trying to say into what you can say. Do you understand? It is like trying to describe a dream.'

'I see what you are getting at, it sort of slips through the fingers of your mind and the harder you try the more mixed up you get until whoever you are telling gives up and thinks you're potty.' Paul said, nodding his head and staring out of the window at the misty, distant hills.

'What about lunch then? Shall I conjure you an omelette with some of those mushrooms or do you have to go home to your parents?' Diana picked up their empty cups and went to the kitchen.

Paul followed 'No, they're gone off to the big bad city, if Exeter is like that, and left me to starve, like your dog. Do you ever feed her? She seems to give the impression no-one gives her any dinner.' Paul looked around for the dog.

'She gets tea and biscuits when I get up and a dish of meat and meal at 6 o'clock. She shouldn't be too fat or she will be lazy.' Diana said

Clover, who had been lying quietly all this time beside the Aga, knowing she was being discussed, came up to the table where they sat and put her nose on Paul's knee. He patted her soft dark fur and silky black ears whilst she tried to lick his hand and snuffle her cold, wet nose against his wrist, her tail beating the floor.

'Soppy dog,' he said, and then to Diana 'Mum says I'll eat anything so long as it isn't another of your potions 'cos I've never tried eye of bat or toe of newt and that.'

Diana lifted one of the lids of the Aga and set down a great iron frying pan into which she poured a little oil. It soon began to sizzle as she chopped up bacon and some of the new mushrooms and tossed them in. Beating up some eggs she talked to Paul as she cooked.

'Lots of those recipes from Shakespeare and so on are names of herbs not grisly bits of animals. There is a tree fungus called Jew's ear and one named Dead Men's Fingers, both all right to eat if they are young. Hounds Tongue is a fern, Mouse Ear is a herb not used much now and so on. They used to think that a plant that was like something would affect that thing. If you had a spotty rash you would be treated with a spotty leaved plant, if a fever something hot...'

'Like curry?' suggested Paul, entering into the spirit of the thing

'Well, Feverfew has a spicy sort of smell. It is all part of what is called 'sympathetic magic'. You act or choose something in sympathy with what you want, like carrying a sprig of mint in your purse to ensure a MINT of money, and a piece of sage for wisdom.'

Soon the lunch was ready and Diana served the omelette onto warmed plates, waiting expectantly to see if Paul was enjoying his share.

'Got any tomato sauce?' he asked through a mouthful, 'Is this mushroom or those golf balls?'

'Both,' Diana replied, finding him the bottle of ketchup, 'the more mushroomy tasting ones are the puffballs.'

There was comparative silence as they tucked into their meal which finished with more of the nutty flapjacks.

'Work,' said Diana suddenly after they had paused their after lunch conversation, 'I've got that wine to make before the elderberries spoil and there's the washing up. You will have to pay for your lunch, you know.'

'Ok, it was a good bite, I'll wash, you wipe, all right.' Paul went to the big sink beneath the window and began to run hot water into the bowl.

'I don't wipe up much,' said Diana, 'plates and things can drip dry. Let me have a fork though, out of the left hand drawer.'

Whilst Paul scoured the greasy plates Diana stripped the glistening black berries off the elder sprigs into a large enamel bowl with a piece of knotted root and some lemons and placed it on the stove to boil.

'What's that then, mandrake or something?' asked Paul seeing the root.

'No, it's ginger root to give a nice flavour. When the berries are soft we will strain the juice, add the sugar and yeast and let it ferment. In a couple of months it will make a dark red wine. If the Romans hadn't introduced grape wine everyone would probably drink either elderberry or blackberry wine as both are very good. When I've done this I will show you something. It is part of a local mystery which I hope to unravel before Christmas.'

'Go on then,' urged Paul impatiently, 'show me.'

Chapter Three
Poems and Puzzles

They had gone into the book-lined room after the work in the kitchen was finished and Diana rummaged for a while in a tall, wooden cupboard in a corner. Eventually she found the bundle she was looking for and brought it to Paul who sat at the big table.

'Read that,' she said, handing him a folded parchment.

Gently, Paul unfolded the stiff brownish parchment and a piece of paper fluttered out of its folds. There was crabbed black writing across it with odd bits added in other, newer looking hands round the edge.

"Beneath ye starrs beneath ye skys..." 'I can't read this old writing, what is it?' said Paul, hesitantly.

'Try the typed version on that bit of paper you dropped.'

"Beneath the stars, beneath the skies
A mighty power of Hallows lies.
Beneath the rivers, springs and seas
The Hallows bide that bring men ease.
Beneath the hearth, beside the fire
Lie Hallows hid for man's desire.
Beneath the roots, within the land
Are Hallows bringing strength to hand.
Beneath the rock, the shining stone
A Hallow lies for you alone"

'It's a sort of riddle which has been passed down through the family. The parchment is probably 18th century or so, but the rhyme is far older. A Hallow is a holy thing which has a magical power and may change its shape or form. I want to find this one "for you alone" because my father thought the shining stone was a diamond, Dymond, like our name, or it might be a shining stone IS the Hallow. It is very complicated. I think it ties in with the Thirteen Treasures of Britain, one of which was the Holy Grail in King Arthur's time,' she paused, brushing dust off the old parchment. 'The poem seems to point to the hiding places beneath rivers and springs, under a hearth and a rock and so on, but beneath the skies could be anywhere, so could within the land. I have a hunch that ancient stone circles and burial mounds are part of this riddle and that the other various clues that the family have unearthed and added to the parchment all tie in somewhere. My great grandfather, David Dymond, found the extra line which says "Look to Michael and he will guide you". That probably means St Michael and the church here is St Michael in the Moor, and all the local Dymonds are buried in that churchyard. Nearly all the men have first names beginning with D, too. If I could unravel enough to fund one of the Hallows it might help find the rest. They are all supposed to be lucky, and if you have them they will grant your heart's desire.'

'Oh,' said Paul, who was almost speechless after this strange explanation, 'it's beyond me. My family are Cockney Sparrows who've lived all over the East End of London. No-one wrote us poems or hid things. Do you think these Hallows are important?' said Paul, peering at the parchment.

Diana said, 'Well, there are very old tales of people questing for various things. There is another aspect which is partly magical, so I don't suppose you will believe it. Tradition has it that there are two forces, one called Chaos and the other Order or Cosmos, sometimes they are termed the Dark and the Light, in myths and legends. Dark is disorder, trouble, war, upheaval and all those things; but light is a force which wants above other things Balance, even with Dark, so that you get day and night, summer and winter and so on. The Dark wants to wipe out the Light so that everything is always chaos, destruction and night without hope of dawn. These Hallows were created by Craftsmen working for Light to act as talismans, like batteries to recharge the Light when Dark succeeds. Magic was tied up in it for it is neutral, a bit like electricity which is useful for heating and cooking but dangerous if the wire insulation is frayed or the plug has no fuse. Magic can be used by both Light and Dark but not against the other side directly. The Hallows would help the Light but they can't because they are hidden in a magical way. If they are found and un-magicked then they will help balance Day and Night and so on.' Diana glanced at her many books.

'But aren't day and night to do with the sun and moon, or something, and the earth turning round?' enquired Paul, looking very puzzled.

'Oh, it is so complicated,' Diana went on, 'I know what I am talking about, but I just can't explain. To me Order matters, that Spring will follow Winter and Summer after Spring and then Autumn and so on. If there was just darkness, life would cease and that would be the end of everything. I want to try to preserve life and light, and by studying old tales find out what our ancestors knew about life and magic, too. Anyway, enough of the philosophy. I want to see if I can find these Hallows, or at least some more information. My family seem to have been after them for hundreds of years and it is time we made some progress.' Diana gathered up the parchment and the typed poem and began to look at them intently. Paul walked round the room, peering at the books crammed into the shelves in no order he could see, and examined the statues and models of animals which were used to prop up the rows. For a while he wandered aimlessly, drawn by the strange and interesting things all around him.

'Look,' he said suddenly, 'I don't know anything about these Hallows but it seems to me that if they are magic things can't you use magic to look for them? I suppose you don't have a crystal ball and a cauldron to go with your broomstick do you, and a black cat? No, Clover wouldn't put up with that! Anyway, you ought to have a spell for finding lost treasure, so long as you don't mind a dragon or two.'

Diana looked at him with her mouth open in amazement

'Brilliant boy,' she smiled 'why on earth didn't I think of that! I have an old book which gives methods of finding treasure and making things appear but I have never tried any of them. I must see what the moon is doing.'

'Nothing,' said Paul, looking out through the glass wall, 'it's still daylight out there, no moon at all.'

'I don't mean at this minute, I mean is she going to help our search?' Diana said, looking at the bookshelf.

After a frantic search hampered by Clover, who thought they were playing a game she could join in, an almanac with pictures of flowers above and dates below scattered with small red writing and signs for full and new moons and planets and zodiac signs was located.

'Saturday. Yes, the moon is waxing – growing at present – will be full on Michaelmas. That ought to help, for increasing light at night means increase of wisdom or hidden knowledge. Let me find that old tome my grandmother got at an auction.'

Diana vanished into her sanctum under the stairs and soon returned with a huge leather covered book, all dusty and smeared with cobwebs. The pages were brownish and it seemed to have been handwritten, with strange diagrams and symbols among the text. After a few moments she found something to help. She read it out to Paul who had a notepad and pen in case it was needed. "To dream of hidden treasure make a magical pillow of herbs of the moon. Take three times three of moon herbs, any sort growing in your land, dried, and put them into a bag of new linen. Take a new candle of bees wax, light it and walk thrice round it with the sun saying "Power of moon's shining beams bring me knowledge in my dreams, Power of gold and power of wealth show what I may gain myself." Place the bag under your pillow and speak to the moon through your open casement, ask for knowledge, then snuff your candle and sleep. Immediately on waking write down all you have dreamed."

'What about that, then?' cried Paul, having noted the details of the spell, 'it's probably a load of old cobblers, but it might help you dream of something. Where are these moon herbs, I suppose you have them, and the candle and so on?'

'I should have no trouble with the herbs, I have dried supplies of all the ones from the garden over the last few years. Bees wax candles ought to be in the kitchen dresser and I have some new linen that I bought in a sale and haven't needed yet. I know herbs of the moon include clary, goosegrass, lily, moonwort, poppy, wormwood, wallflower, willow, iris and wintergreen. I can find a sample of nine of those without too much effort and I can make a bag...'

'Two bags,' said Paul firmly, 'I want one as well. If you are trying magic I don't want to be left out. Mum won't mind me having a candle, I don't suppose, and two heads are better than one, as the monster said to himself.'

Diana smiled and explained the sewing might take a while.

'Why don't you take Clover for a run down to the river and back?' asked Diana. 'Follow this lane until you come to the stile by the bridge, then go along the bank until you get to the second gate into a field, follow along the hedge and it comes out further along there. I don't think there are any cattle in there at present, but you will find her collar and lead in the porch, end hook by the door. Come here, dog.' Clover came to her mistress's knee immediately, mouth open in a tongue-lolling grin, tail wagging nineteen to the dozen. 'Go with Paul, be good and don't fall in the river. Go on, then.'

With no further ado they were off, Paul collected the lead and put Clover's leather collar on, fitting it to the worn hole with the buckle.

'Heel.' he said sharply as they came through the gate into the lane but there was no sign of any traffic. If three cars passed through that village in a day they thought it was a traffic jam, Paul imagined.

As soon as he had gone Diana went into her work room under the stairs and fetched the dried herbs and linen and a while later she had made two bags, each about a foot square, and after mixing a handful of each of the nine different herbs together in a big bowl, she stuffed the bags. When Paul and Clover came back, panting for a drink, she only had to finish the bags with a piece of red ribbon, which she explained to Paul, as he sniffed the mixture with interest, was a traditional magical way of sealing a spell. Over a glass of cold juice they discussed how to perform the rest of the spell and decided to try it as it came to them. Diana gave Paul a new white candle set into a short holder and a box of matches and the small pillow of herbs. He picked up his box of mushrooms and set off home in time to make his parents a cup of tea when they got back from Exeter.

'What a strange turn of events,' he thought to himself, as he walked between the tall hedges in the village lanes, set up on broad stone banks, now covered with late summer flowers. 'Mixed up with ancient poems, quests for hallows and magic herb pillows. What next, I wonder?'

He arrived home about half an hour before his father's car drew up and his mother immediately began to order him about, helping with stowing the shopping, putting things into the freezer, making tea and generally bustling about.

In order to avoid unnecessary conversation he took the notes he had made on the tree branches, and the wilted specimens themselves, into the front room and set about his project.

'You're not ill, are you?' his mother asked as he went up to bed without a murmur, the first time she asked. 'You haven't been eating toadstools and getting poisoned? The ones you showed me looked ok but goodness knows what you and that Mrs Dymond were eating earlier.'

'I'm all right. Just tired, it must be all this fresh air and exercise. I did take her dog for a long walk this afternoon, down by the river and through the fields...'

'You haven't been and fallen in the river then, and got a chill?' his mother scolded. 'I always warned you not to go near running water, the canal was bad enough.'

'No, Mum, I am ok. You aren't making any hot chocolate though, are you?'

'I am not, nor am I traipsing up those stairs again until bed time,' his mother called, 'there's water in the bathroom if you're thirsty.'

'I thought you just warned me off running water. Don't go near it, you said,' said Paul, grinning.

'Now you mind your tongue, my lad, or your Dad will be up there in no time. Get to sleep as I suppose you'll be gallivanting off into the fields again tomorrow, not helping me in this big garden, or washing the car for your Dad...' her voice faded as she went back to stare at a travel TV programme with his father.

Paul opened his window wide and leaned out. By bending to one side he could see the crescent of the moon partly hidden by scudding clouds. After shutting his door he put the candle in its holder in the middle of the floor, placed the herb bag under his pillow and, taking the bit of paper on which he had copied the rhyme from his jeans pocket, he walked solemnly round to face the window as the half moon crept into view. He lit the candle and walking as quietly as he could circled the flame three times, clockwise, as the old book had said. He read the words under his breath as he did so, again three times as Diana had told him spells often go in threes.

After snuffing the candle and waving his dressing gown about to disperse the smell he hopped into bed. From where he lay he could see the shining shape of the moon's half circle creep gradually across his open window

'Please help us,' he said silently, feeling a bit of a fool, 'let us find these treasured Hallows and help me understand this Light and Dark business.'

The herbs warmed up as he leaned on them, and the strange scent oozed over him, lulling and calming, until he fell asleep.

'Please let me dream of something magical,' he thought as his eyes closed.

A Unicorn seemed to be standing at the end of his bed with a wild rose in its mouth.

Chapter Four
The Land of Legend

'Hello, Master Paul,' said the Unicorn, without moving his lips, 'I have come to take you to the Land of Legend to study the Matter of Myths and the Truth of Tales.'

Paul examined him closely, his head, like that of a small horse was a silvery grey, not shining white fur like Clover, but with purplish shadows. His mane was long and hung in waves down one side of his neck and in the middle of his forehead stood a single, twisted bright golden horn about a foot long. Paul was astounded and was just about to ask a question when the Unicorn answered him.

'You may not speak, nor may you interfere in anything you see. If you need to have an explanation I will give it to you.'

As he spoke he ate the sprig of wild rose delicately, like a donkey eating thistles, and managed it all without pricking his mouth.

'Come on, across my back you will find a cloak, wrap yourself in it and climb on my back and we will be off.'

Although he wasn't talking as humans do, Paul considered his words and decided he had a welsh accent. Scrambling over his bed covers he found it was easy to reach the dark, midnight blue cloak lined with something sparkly like starlight. He put it round his shoulders and fastened the buckle of silver which held it in place. He then slid onto the Unicorn's smooth, warm back, grasped a double handful of his mane and, with no further ado, they were off.

With a great leap the Unicorn went straight through the window and shot into the sky which thudded under his hooves as if he were galloping on over a mown lawn. Paul, who had never ridden anything except a seaside donkey, gripped hard with his knees and hung onto the Unicorn's mane. He was at first frightened and then thrilled as they thundered through the sky. It was still night and the land, if it was land below them, was just shadows and forms but gradually the light in the sky began to increase and they dropped lower on that invisible road until they were on the earth again. The Unicorn slowed his pace to a gentle walk and Paul looked around him, discovering they had reached a deep, dark winter forest of huge ancient trees, almost bare and with patches of snow glimmering in the hollows. He was not cold but drew the cloak tightly round him as a gesture.

'I am going to show you the story of the year from which many other myths and tales have grown,' said the Unicorn, 'watch with your eyes and your heart but do not speak nor take any part in what happens. It is not allowed to alter the archetype, the structure of the story of it would change the whole of the future, the past to you. Get down now, follow this path to a clearing. If you need me, imagine me beside you and I will come. Farewell.' The Unicorn turned and trotted off among the trees, Paul noticed the switch at the end of his tail was golden.

Following the path Paul soon came to a clearing in which stood a great chair, covered with white silk where people were arriving dressed in ancient costume. The men mostly wore short tunics and coloured tights and the women wore long gowns of bright fabrics, with shorter cloaks over the top. Some folk wore jewels and gold chains which flashed and sparkled in the dawn light, others were poorer people wearing greys, greens and duns of natural dyes.

Suddenly, there was a blast of horn music and all the throng parted to make a path down the centre to the throne. With a soft rustle a stately, tall woman walked through the crowd up to the great chair and settled herself. She was clad in a dark, all enveloping mantle which was hooded and even though her face was half hidden Paul knew she was beautiful. As the throng of folk settled itself before her she stood up and began to unfasten the dark cloak. Slowly she drew it back from her skirt which was the softest, palest green, like beech leaves new opened against the sun. As her green robe was disclosed so the encircling trees broke into leaf and the sun began to rise. Paul could now see that her mantle was the deepest brown imaginable, like peat from a deep pit. Her skirt was green but it was caught in at the waist with a chain of daisies and as this was revealed Paul could see springing up through the winter mould all round him the first spring flowers. Snowdrops, windflowers, primroses, pink cuckoopint, crocuses purple, white and gold, tiny violets and a warm wind blew the scents about him. Then her mantle was finally cast aside and he could see she was smiling.

Her hair was dark and shot with reddish lights and her eyes were like violets, the top of her dress was all colours, embroidered with flowers and fruits and she had a necklace of glinting stones, set in silver, that shone like moonlight. Many folk in the throng picked flowers and took them to offer them, kneeling at her feet and Paul wanted to do the same but not being sure how far the Unicorn's words applied he did not like to act. Suddenly there was another horn call and a band of men in tunics and jackets and tights of various shades of green ran into the clearing. The leader, a tall stern-looking man, carried a long bow but a sword was sheathed at his side. as he doffed his hat before the throne she said 'Greetings, Robin'

He replied 'My Lady, I have come to the hunt. Will you honour us with your presence?'

Without a word she rose and, flinging aside the flowers, ran swiftly into a thicket of hawthorn which burst into a foam of scented white may blossom. With a cry, Robin Hood and his men followed, hallooing through the trees. Paul ran as fast as he could in order not to lose sight of the hunters but their green and brown garb soon merged with the trees and bushes and he found himself alone. After a pause to get his breath back he thought of the Unicorn and remembered his words. Calling to mind the clearest picture of him he could, as he had first seen him, eating the rose, Paul concentrated on the picture. with no sound he found the Unicorn standing beside him, again nibbling a frond of flowers. 'Come on,' he said, trotting to stand beside a fallen tree so that Paul could mount, 'they won't be far away, this forest doesn't last long.'

In a few moments of hair raising dodging through the thick forest they came upon the hunters. Some were building a fire in a clearing and others were still in the woods hallooing and blowing their horns. Suddenly a large white form burst into the circle, just as the bonfire caught and flames and white smoke swept upwards. The hunters closed in round their quarry, a great white hind, the colour of snow with eyes that glowed like cherries. Robin Hood was close behind and all the huntsmen chivvied the deer, driving her closer to the fire. Finally with a great leap she cleared the flames with Robin right behind her. As they landed safe on the other side Paul was amazed to see the deer had changed into the lady who had made the land flower. Hand in hand she and Robin ran into the thicket of blossoming hawthorn, his merry men, cheering and laughing faded too. Whether they just merged with the trees or their camouflage colouring hid them Paul did not know but soon he was alone again except for the Unicorn.

'Onward,' said the silvery beast, 'to the next part of the story. It won't be a moment.'

They came to the edge of the forest where there was a lake, and in the distance the shadowy form of a castle, dark against a pale morning sky. There was a cold wind blowing when a small boat, rowed by a figure in a faded grey cloak came to the beach not far from them. As he clambered ashore he gently lifted a bundle from the boat, which squirmed and seemed to whimper as if it were alive. The old man looked around for a moment then let out a piercing whistle, three sharp blasts falling in tone, as you might whistle your dog. There was a pause and a thud of hooves and two horses came out of the woods. On one was a girl but the other was riderless. Handing up his bundle to the girl the old man said 'take him to the forest and guard him. He is the king's son, rightwise born of his queen but men may doubt him. He shall be the king that was and the king that is to be. Nurture him and keep him safe and I will bring him here again to take his place as a Light to the people.'

Without another word he mounted his horse and galloped away along the edge of the lake. The girl slightly unwrapped the bundle and cooed and chattered to the babe within the wrappings, 'come on then my beauty.' and soon she and her mount faded into the woods.

Time seemed to pass as the Unicorn browsed on some honeysuckle. Paul wandered by the lake, watching the light change and fish jump from its still waters. There was a flurry and splash and a young boy, closely followed by another rushed into the water, splashing and laughing as they ducked one another and chased about on the edge of the lake. After a few moments they ran back into the forest and soon two older boys came, this time swimming strongly out into the lake and back. On shore they wrestled and struggled before returning to the woods. A third pair came out and Paul was convinced these were either sets of brothers or the same lads, aging before his eyes. This time they rode large horses, one grey, the other chestnut, and they fought with sharp swords for he could see the sparks and hear the ring and clash of steel on steel.

There was another stir on the edge of the forest and an old horse appeared and on it's back the man in the faded grey cloak, looking much the same. His hood was thrown back and for a time he sat on his horse, watching. His hair and beard were quite white, but as he looked around, seeming to nod to the Unicorn, Paul saw a sparkle in his eyes that told of humour and fun.

'Enough,' he cried, 'I have a sterner test for you. Bedwyr, sound your horn and let the people come.' The lad on the chestnut horse sheathed his sword and took a small horn from his belt and blew a short call. Soon folk began to arrive from all over the place. Foresters and woodcutters, dames with little children, regal folk in silks and jewels with hawks on their wrists, farmfolk and dairy maids. A baker with a tray of bread, and as this fellow passed close to the Unicorn he lowered his horn and neatly speared a small loaf and passed it to Paul. The bread was still warm and tasted nutty and fresh. The Unicorn ate a piece of the soft inside but refused the crunchy crust.

Soon there was a great throng of people all craning and pushing to see what was going on but the old man stood a little apart, talking seriously to the lad with the white horse. Paul edged round to listen.

'This is your moment to prove your worth, your land is almost unprotected, her kind is dying with no known heir, swords gather rust whilst their owners quarrel about land or taxes and fight their neighbours whilst a greater, darker foe gathers across the water. Before these people you have to prove you can lead them, for you are Arthur, rightful king of this land in the stead of Pendragon, Uther the king who lies dying and helpless. There is a test here beside the lake to show that you, and you alone have the strength to lead this land in war, the intelligence to guide her people in peace. Come.'

The old grey man strode through the crowd to a space at the edge of the wood and climbed onto the stump of a fallen tree.

'Hearken,' he cried to the watching people. There was a mutter through the crowd 'Merlin, Merlin, a wonder, give us a wonder...'

'Hearken to me,' he cried again, but the murmur continued, drowning his words. Reading into a pouch which hung at his belt he drew something forth and threw it up, over the heads of the crowd. There was a great bang and a shower of sparks raining down on their upturned faces. Silence fell.

'I have gathered you here today to show you your new king, Arthur. Uther Pendragon lies dying of his wounds gained in fighting for your country and he has no known son, yet here is Arthur, born of Igern his queen, and reared, hidden in the dark forests. He is now ready to take up the sword in defence of the land and lead you to victory over the dark forces which would cover these green fields and forests. I will prove his strength. Woodman, bring me your axe.'

Without a word a forester came forward carrying an axe over his shoulder. Merlin drew him aside to a clump of bushes and trees at the edge of the forest and showed him what to cut. Chopping down small saplings and thicker tree trunks alike, his keen blade soon lay bare the face of a great rock which had been deeply covered with growth. In the centre of the rock, in a cleft running into its heart stood the hilt of a sword, still bright from the protection of the covering leaves. Everyone gasped, not knowing about this strange thing which had been hidden nearby for many a long year.

'That sword was struck into the rock by a mighty king who ruled these lands before the fathers of your fathers lived. He could not take it with him after his last battle but left it here for his successor. He knew no ordinary man should draw it forth, only he who had a right to lead this land, defend it from its enemies, cast back the darkness of doubt and despair. Now we have a great need for such a one. If there is any man here who feels he has the right to lead, to be king in war and in peace, let him claim this blade, draw it forth and declare himself. No one will doubt his right.'

A muttering ran through the crowd, a retelling of old tales of kings and powers and from the great throng several tall and tough looking men came forward. Each in turn gripped the sword hilt in the crack of rock and heaved and strained. None could budge it an inch. When all that had wanted a go had their turn, some trying two of three times, Merlin spoke to Arthur who stepped forward.

'If it is my right that I should take this sword, I will free it,' he cried aloud, and bracing his foot on the rock and grasping its carved hilt in both hands he threw his weight against it and heaved. For a moment he struggled, the whole crowd still and holding its breath, then with a slither and chime the shining blade slid out of the rock. A resounding cheer went up from the throats of all present. Women wept and men roared and slapped each other on the back. Arthur climbed to the top of the rock and held out his arms.

'People, will you accept me as your king in the stead of my father Uther who until this day I did not know? Will you permit me untried and young to be your battle lord?'

'Aye,' they all yelled, 'aye, Arthur, aye.'

As he stood above them the sun broke through the misty clouds, in its full noon brightness, so he stood shining before his people like a flame of white fire, and as he stepped down his shadow seemed to hang in the air behind him and step down too, a dark echo of his own light. Only Merlin, Paul and the Unicorn seemed to see this. There was another flurry from the forest as a man mounted on a weary and sweat streaked horse galloped into the clearing. 'Uther is dead,' he cried, 'the king is dead, who shall lead us now?'

He was helped from his horse and as a groom led it away someone took him to Arthur and told him of his sword. A hawk hovered over the clearing and then was gone into the blue. It now seemed to be full summer, the trees green and leafy, the forest floor banked with wild flowers and fruits. Birds sang but in the distance came the sound of clashing swords and the thunder of galloping horses. Yells and screams were carried on the wind and sometimes ragged, weary figures staggered past the place where Paul and the Unicorn stood waiting. Eventually it grew quieter and the sounds of harp music and laughter rang through the woods. A party of men and women rode gently through the trees, and among them was Arthur and a woman in purple and gold. Beside her rode Bedwyr and all chatted and sang in the afternoon light.

Later on Arthur in his silver mail rode alone and another knight in green riding a pale horse, which among the thick foliage also seemed green, emerged. The Green Knight charged at Arthur with his great sword raised, Arthur tore his own blade from its scabbard and defended himself. With clangs and clashes their blades struck and the horses, trained for war, sidled and backed to the smallest signal from their riders. With a great cross handed blow Arthur caught the other knight across the shoulder and tumbled him from his saddle. Jumping from his own horse Arthur fought on, matching the other blow for blow, until his green enemy lay as his feet, his sword struck from his hand. Arthur stood over him the shining blade of his sword upraised.

'As you offered no challenge you need no mercy,' and without another word he struck off the Green Knight's head. Paul gasped, but was even more astonished when the body of the Green Knight rolled over, picked up his head and set it above his shoulders, bowed to Arthur and caught his green horse.

'I am a wonder, the green one who dies and rises again. There are many such as me in this forest. Lest your knights grow bored and wary to peace we are to be sought. The white stag will run from you, the red eared hound quest for you, giants and strange beings will dwell in this place for your company to seek. Each of us has a Hallow, a holy thing which is the real prize. If you gather your knights only the best, the greatest, the strongest will gain a true token. Each one who wins a victory will lose something he holds dear. Whilst you fought me, Guinevere, your queen, was carried off by your dearest friend. You will regain her body but you have lost her heart. She too has lost, for she will bear no children.' Raising his sword in salute the green knight fled into the woods and Arthur in a wrath leapt upon his stallion and turned and rode away.

The leaves began to fall in the forest and shadows flitted through as the questing knights sought the strange creatures and the treasures that the green knight had promised. One knight, seeming no older than a boy, riding a bony old horse passed by, his face alight with some inner joy, and bundled in a fold of his cloak some smallish thing which burned like an arc lamp, illuming the darkening forest as the leaves fluttered about him. Paul could almost feel his exhilaration.

The Unicorn was beside him again and they set off, following the last rider until they came to a great hall, set up amid the spreading branches of the trees. Still wrapped in his dark cloak Paul looked very like one of the folk of the place and he followed others who were entering the door. The Unicorn had vanished again but Paul was interested to see what was going on and did not mind adventuring alone. Inside the hall the grey stone walls were hung with bright tapestries and a huge fire blazed at one end. In the centre of the hall stood a great circular table and around it were seated many of the knights, each one having some object, wrapped in cloth before him. The other ordinary folk seemed to have vanished but no-one took any notice of Paul, almost as if they couldn't see him.

Arthur sat in an elaborately carved and decorated throne and beside him stood Merlin. The conversation died and it was very quiet, silent but for the crackle of burning logs and the sound of the wind through the unglazed windows.

'My Lords,' said Merlin gently to the gathered company, 'you have done great deeds, fought against great odds and seen many wonders. Each of you has won a valuable prize yet each has lost something also. If you rest your arms will grow weaker but your tempers hotter. Brother will quarrel with brother, kin attack kin, for the dark force which breeds in war festers in peace until that peace is broken. This age of peace one by battle and deed of arms cannot long remain, you will need your spears and warhorses again ere long, but you have a duty yet to perform concerning the Hallows which you have brought to Arthur's hall. Each must be taken and hidden and surrounded with spells so that in ages to come other seekers may go on a quest and rediscover these Hallows, these talismans of protection which will guard the spirit of this land. Each of you needed courage and wit to attain your prizes, use those skills to place them safe from harm until their light shall be needed again, or until seekers with keenness and strength shall find them.

This land will see wonders beyond your dreams, but it shall fall under a dark spell. Doubt, despair, anger, boredom and confusion may dwell here and the powers of chaos, disorder and darkness fill the hearts of the people. The light of these Hallows will be needed again then. To each of you I will give a magical powder which will hide and disguise the Hallow, protect it from common thieves, keep it from decay until it is brought into the light of day again.

To you Arthur I say your mightiest enemy has not yet been quelled, you have brought peace but in it the seeds of war, you have founded a company of perfect knights whose acts will be long remembered, yet they have grown weary of perfection and will seek other quarry in the land. Always there are opposite forces working in the land, like day and night, Summer and Winter. Whilst they are in harmony of balance all is well but when the dark overtakes the light every weapon in the armoury of man will be needed to set matters to rights.'

The hall grew dark and there was muttering round the table as the knights drew together. Only the cloth covered Hallows that lay before them glowed with a misty light, and Arthur's great sword which lay drawn on the table before him, burned like a laser of sparkling white fire. Paul walked quietly from the hall, wondering what it all meant. As he turned back into the forest to look for the Unicorn a dove or pigeon flew past him and close behind was a hawk, a blue-grey Merlin. Watching their flight he saw them fly straight into a cave in some fallen rocks behind the hall. As he moved nearer there was a great crash of thunder and flash of lightening above him. From the pile of stones flew the dove, pale against the thunder dark sky, but the Merlin did not appear from the tumbled rocks.

Walking back towards the lake shore and calling to mind the picture of the Unicorn, Paul soon came out of the trees. The Unicorn stood waiting for him, silvery and mysterious against the evening dim waters of the lake. There was mist in the air and the smell of autumn as they waited on the shore. Suddenly from the trees burst two struggling shapes, one silver-bright, the other shadow-dark, armed knights with great swords. Circling each other warily they began to fight. Clangs and clashes of sword on armour, blade on blade were echoed by flashes of lightening and roars of thunder from a sky which shed no tears of rain. Blow followed blow, each knight in turn falling to his knees then struggling to his feet again, first the black knight then the white. Paul could hear them panting and groaning as the slashes struck through mail and plate. It grew darker as the rolling masses of grey cloud shrouded the setting sun yet gleams of red light sought out the combatants so that you could not tell if it was red light or blood which bathed their battling forms. With a great cry the silvery knight raised his sword and changing a downward blow into a side sweep at the last moment lunged at his foe. The glittering blade struck home, but his enemy, in falling brought down his blade on the silver helmet and both crashed to the ground, motionless. From the forest rushed the other knights but there seemed nothing they could do. The silver knight they lifted tenderly but before they could return to his hall a boat had drawn up silently near to them and three dark figures spoke with the knights so that they placed the injured silver knight into the board. Slowly it moved off across the misty water but even in the darkness there was a glitter of light, a brilliant shaft of whiteness upheld. Faintly across the still water a voice called out,

'I am gone to the island of apples but I will return with the light. Guard the flame that I have set in your hearts that your children's children may find hope in darkness.'

The gleaming blade shone but the arm that held it grew weak and it sagged over the edge of the black boat, finally dropping from a feeble hand into the still, deep water without a splash. The dim shape swirled and faded, the silent oars propelled it away, beyond the knowledge of man. Bedwyr stood helpless at the edge of the lake watching the shadow fade across the lake, he said quietly, 'There shall be a mystery forever about the grave of Arthur, the king who was and shall come again.' and he began to weep. From the forest the sound of chanting arose, 'He is gone, the good king who brought us the light, who turned back the foe and made our fields green. He is gone, Arthur the young, the bright knight who fought the darkness.' A cavalcade of ghostly figures walked along the shore of the lake, into the darkness, knights in armour, women with children, ancient shadows from all times of the land, departing in the wake of their king to a place beyond time.

'There is one more thing,' said the Unicorn at Paul's side, 'one last part to this story which may be familiar to you,' and he led Paul back into the forest, past the hall to a low cattle shed. It stood in a clearing and now the clouds had fled there were many stars, glittering with frost brightness. One in particular seemed to hang brilliant and still above the clearing, and even the light of the rising moon seemed dim. Inside the shed there were shadows against a small lamp, figures standing around in the straw. In the middle was a young woman, and Paul gasped, surely this was the beautiful lady he had seen before, now clothed in blue of a summer sky with a white cloth, hiding her hair. In her arms she held a tiny baby which cried and murmured as she rocked it. There was a strange light here too, and Paul was reminded of the young knight on the old horse who had grasped some glowing secret thing in his cloak. The Unicorn spoke again, quietly 'There is always a child of promise, even in the darkest night. In doubt and despair is born hope, in sadness is born courage, in the depth of winter is born the promise of spring. Come.'

They left the shed and the gleaming light and walked through the trees and soon they came upon other hurrying folk, hastening towards a throne set among the trees, covered with white rugs. A cry went up from their throats, 'She is coming...' Turning away from the gathering people the Unicorn took him back to the short of the lake.

'As you have kept your silent, and have not interfered with the pattern of the turning year, I can grant you a small reward. The quest which King Arthur and his knights made famous is still going on, even in your world. Anyone who believes himself to be capable of the quest, no matter where or when, can hope to find one of the Hallows, most suited to him or her, or help another in such a quest. Pick up a pebble from this beach and show it to me.'

Paul looked down around his feet in the rising light of dawn. Pebbles gleamed wetly after the mist had washed over them, brown and grey, red and black, and here and there one which sparkled white. Pausing for only a moment he selected a white one and showed it to the Unicorn. It was shaped like a pear drop and about one inch long and felt cold and smooth to his fingers. Without knowing why he felt he liked the stone. The Unicorn regarded it for a moment then gently lowered his head until the tip of his horn touched it. Paul almost jumped as it began to tingle on his outstretched palm.

'This will now be a talisman,' the Unicorn said, 'if you spin it on the ground the pointed end will point to home, and if danger is near it will feel hot. If you are close to one of the Hallows it will tingle but only you, or anyone you give it to on purpose, will feel these things. Look after it, for you will not return to this place. Can you climb onto my back?'

'Yes,' said Paul at last, glad to end his silence. From a tree stump he clambered onto the Unicorn's smooth, silver back, grasped his thick mane in both hands and they were off, galloping into the night. Soon the Unicorn gave a great leap, there was a soft thud as Paul landed on his bed. The Unicorn took the cloak in his teeth as soon as Paul had unfastened it, flicked his head to lay it across his back and was gone. A welsh voice seemed to be calling 'Farewell, good luck with your quest.'

It was very dark and quiet and, except for a slight rustle of wind in the rose bush outside his window Paul could hear nothing. He yawned and snuggled down under his quilt. In a moment or two he was awoken by the sound of the paperboy slamming the front gate and the light of the early sunshine making strange patterns through the roseleaves on his bedroom wall. Downstairs he could hear his mother putting plates on the table with a clatter and the rising shriek as the kettle worked itself up to boil. There was a strange smell, part roses and part something else, a sharper, spicier, more sinister smell, as if greenness had a smell of its own. Reaching under his pillow Paul found the herb bag, it crumbled and crackled in his fingers.

'Weird,' he thought to himself, 'it didn't half make me sleep.' He yawned and stretched and decided that as it was a nice sunny day he ought to make the best of it.

'Paul, you getting up,' his mother called up the stairs, 'do you want a cooked breakfast? There's all these mushrooms to have with bacon if you like, or you can have wheatybrix.'

'Mushrooms, please, Mum, and a chunk of fried bread. Got any tomatoes or an egg or two? This country air makes me starving.'

He put his foot out of the bed and it touched something cold and smooth lying on the floor beside his bed. He looked down, astonished, and there was a shiny white pebble which seemed to tingle as his bare foot touched it.

'Oh,' he said to himself, 'I did have a dream last night. Better get a bit of paper and write it down. Now, what happened?'

As he ate the tasty cooked breakfast his mother set before him he began to remember, a Unicorn and a forest and strange comings and goings. He had to remember it all to tell Diana, it might be important to her quest, and what was it about this white pebble?'

Chapter Five
The Silver Web

'Hi Spadger,' said his father, coming out from behind the Sunday paper, 'you going to clean my car or help your Mum trim the lawn? Can't waste this nice spell of weather, we might go for a run up on the moors after lunch and have a cream tea in one of the villages.'

'Yes, Dad, but I must have another go at my homework, I get lots more done here than I used to in London,' said Paul, trying to think of a good excuse to get out of garden chores. In town he hadn't minded cleaning the car because there wasn't a lot to do, but now he was getting used to the country there were all kinds of places to explore, most of which he would prefer to do alone.

'Look, let me have another bash at this biology project then I'll do the lawn. Don't know about going out this afternoon. If I haven't got enough trees I might have to look for some more samples or old Larky will go on at me. He knows I come from London and don't know much about trees.'

'Well you get on with your homework whilst I do the washing up and then you can give me or your Dad a hand outside.' said his mother, taking away his plate and tea cup almost before they were empty.

Paul retreated into the front room and shut the door. Having had time to gather his thoughts over breakfast he could recall quite large chunks of his night's adventure. It had not seemed like a dream at the time and he still couldn't understand how he had come by the stone which seemed to tingle slightly in his palm. Tearing a few pages out of his rough work book he began to jot down notes on what he could remember about his journey through the forest and by the lake. He knew he would have to think up a reason to go and see Diana and find out what had happened to her. Fortunately, he had already completed his project but his scribbling looked like homework when his mother looked in on him during the morning. Suddenly he remembered the herb pillow and the candle still on his bedside table, which might take some explaining to his mother if she found them whilst looking for washing. He dashed upstairs and grabbing the offending objects shoved them into the drawer of his hobbies cupboard, which was full of half made plastic models, boxed games that were only played at Christmas and all manner of oddments which had no other home.

Still unable to think of an excuse to visit Diana he had to go down into the garden and help his mother with the lawn. She had already mowed it with an electric mower but all the long stalks round the edge needed trimming with a long handled pair of bent shears which cut at right angles. They were heavy and a bit too long for Paul and made his arms ache, but he battled on, knowing that if he was doing what he was told his parents would have no excuse to stop him going out later, or so he hoped. His mother, dressed in an old but brightly coloured dress was scrabbling about under the rose bushes, pulling out weeds and dead leaves.

'Paul, give us a hand here,' she called, 'I've got to prune these roses and I need a hand to steady the bits I cut off.'

Paul cut the last grass edge and then went to help. Grasping the twisted prickly branches, which obviously hadn't been touched for years was quite a task, and after a while his father took a hand, bringing a small saw to get through the really thick bits. His mother quickly vanished into the kitchen where the clattering of pots and tasty smelling steam coming from the open window foretold a nice lunch to follow soon.

'Paul, do you know what mint looks like?' she called, 'I want some for sauce, see if you can find any. Your Dad can help.'

It didn't take Paul long to discover a great cluster of dark green leaves growing against the fence, he recognised them from Diana's garden and picking some he could smell the refreshing minty smell. His father inspected his find.

'That looks ok to me,' he said, 'your Mrs Dymond showing you the plants then? I hear in the village she is a great one for herbal teas and whatnot. Take these to you Mum and tell her I'm ready for a good lunch any minute now.' His father pottered off down the garden with a great bundle of rose cuttings wrapped in an old sack.

Paul took the mint into the kitchen where his mother quickly chopped it with a sprinkle of sugar then put it into a small green glass jug with a drop of hot water and some vinegar.

'Give that a stir,' she said, handing the jug to Paul, 'while I turn over the roast potatoes.' She bent to the oven and a wave of hot tasty smelling air came from inside.

Soon lunch was ready, a great joint of lamb, roast potatoes, green beans from their neighbours garden and small carrots. This was followed by apple crumble with thick Devon cream. Paul was already beginning to like living in the country for they had eaten fruit or really tasty vegetables every day, making a change from the wilted cabbages from the local market or frozen veg.

Paul was still trying to think of a good reason to go to visit Diana when, as he helped wash the lunch plates his mother said, 'That dog you took out, Clover isn't it, would it eat this? She held out the bone from the middle of the joint, 'You can take it if you want, and if you don't eat it the dog probably will.'

'Yes, please,' said Paul, who loved to gnaw any bone that came his way, 'I'll give it a chew and then offer it to Clover, if Diana will let me. Can I go now?' he said as he picked up the plastic bag with the bone in and took his jacket from behind the kitchen door.

'Don't be late, then, and if you're in the way, come home again. I'll not have you being a nuisance to other folk. Tea will be at 5.30.'

Paul was off, only waiting to stuff the notes into his pocket. As he trotted down the lane he hoped that Diana was in, and that she had finished lunch. He knocked on the back door but his knocking was met with silence instead of the barks from Clover that he had expected. Paul did not want to go home to face more gardening so he sat on the doorstep and taking the lamb bone from its bag, began to chew the juicy meat which his mother had generously left on it. After a few minutes there was a scuffle of feet and Clover, closely followed by Diana, came through the gate.

'I say, what have we here, a starving vagabond, gnawing a bone on my doorstep. I didn't expect to be entertaining trolls for tea!' Diana was laughing, as she watched Paul struggle to his feet, somewhat hampered by his snack.

'Mum thought Clover might like this bone, from the joint, but as you weren't here I was deciding what to do...'

'Food for thought, eh?' said Diana, with a laugh, 'Well, come in, the door's not locked. No doubt Clover will make short work of that, if you are sure you can spare it.' Diana led the way into the kitchen and Clover nosed around Paul, a begging look in her eyes. Paul gave the bone to Diana who made certain there were no rough edges to hurt her dog, then making Clover sit and beg for it she gave it to her, opening the door to usher dog and bone into the garden.

'If she wants to bury it I would rather it wasn't under the sofa cushion or the mat in the hall,' said Diana, knowing her pet's peculiar habits. 'Would you like a cup of coffee or a cold drink?' she asked Paul.

'Some fruit juice, please, it's still jolly warm for September.'

'I've got some plum juice, like to try that?' Paul nodded and was soon given a big glass of cloudy purple juice which tasted of plums but nicer.

'I didn't half dream last night,' said Paul, 'did your pillow do anything to you?'

'Yes, it did. That is why I went out, to get my new map back from the vicar. He borrowed it a month ago. Had to catch him at lunch because he is off to another village church this afternoon, a christening or something.' Diana held out the new, shiny covered ordnance survey map.

'First you tell me what happened to you, then I will explain what I learned. If anything ties up it might be a further clue, like a jigsaw.'

Paul pulled the scribbled notes from his pocket and gave them to Diana, hoping she could understand what he had written. For a few moments he sipped his drink and then picking up the map carefully unfolded it and spread it on the table, taking a large fossil snail, a heavy book, a piece of sea washed driftwood and a flat river pebble, all of which were lying about, to hold down the corners. He had been taught a bit about maps at school but this had lots of green for woods and brown for high land as it showed most of Dartmoor with its villages clustering round the edges. Paul soon found Micklehampton and traced the roads and lanes which he had just begun to know on foot. He could see the steep hills which were visible from his bedroom and read their names, Ashburn Tor was the highest point. The whole area seemed to be peppered with ancient monuments, standing stones, hut circles, field systems but there were few roads across the great Dartmoor Forest, nor were there any villages across those windy uplands, except the ancient ones.

Diana read his notes without too much difficulty and agreed that it had indeed been a hectic night. She told him she knew most of the legends which he had witnessed and that his dream had been a mixture of the pagan festivals of the year, ones that the country folk used to celebrate long ago mixed up with the King Arthur story, parts of which Paul had read before. The Lady he had seen was the original Mother Nature who has many disguises and appears in many religions, as at the end she seemed to be the Virgin Mary with the holy child and the great star. There were very old stories of other holy ladies, Diana explained, who had feasts at different times of year, many of which had become saint's days now. It was like peeling an onion, you took off one set of stories with their named heroes and heroines and underneath was another lot, the same sort of people but with different names or attributes. It was very complicated.

'It does match up with some of the things I dreamed,' she said at last, 'I seemed to be flying high above here and could see points of light and lines, just like a great silver web spread out across the whole of the land, or a huge wheel. Here and there were clusters of lights like stars, and some places were very dark, as if they sent out beams of darkness instead of light. I began to see that the wheel was to do with the year, like a round calendar, and that the bright spots were ancient places, good places where kindly folk live or old stones on the moor. The dark places were evil, bogs or abandoned cottages, places where there had been accidents or strange tales of ghosts. Somehow I have to try and find the dark places and make them light, so that the pattern can be whole. I seemed to be given a small lamp with a flickering flame which I have to keep alight out of doors on a windy night. It was very difficult to do but I knew it was important, then that dog barked at someone in the road and I woke up with a voice saying "your grandfather put a light up the chimney..." Perhaps we had better take a look, I will fetch a torch.'

In a moment Diana returned with a rubber-covered torch in her hand and peered up the great chimney whose spanning beam was carved with a diamond shape and DD inside, the family's initials. With a clatter the logs and pine cones fell off the hearth as she scrambled onto them her head and shoulders vanishing inside the chimney. There was a scrabbling and muttering which Paul couldn't understand then a thud as a broken brick fell at his feet. More muffled words followed and a mist of soot began to rain down around Diana. There was one more shower of bits of brickwork, dust and charred sticks and she struggled backwards out of the fireplace, covered in smut but holding something in her left hand. The torch still shone on her blackened face.

'Good thing I didn't suggest you went up that chimney, your mother wouldn't let you visit me if you came back looking like this. I better go and change.' She left Paul, taking with her the treasure from the chimney and leaving a trail of black across the carpet.

It didn't take Diana long to change into clean clothes, and brush the worst of the soot from her hair, and rinse her hands and face. She was wiping a cloth over her find when she came back to Paul.

'Look,' she said holding out the object.

Paul took it gingerly and going over to the window examined her find. It was an old pottery lamp made of something like flowerpot-coloured clay but it was bigger than some Paul had seen in a museum. On the top was embossed a figure of someone in armour standing on a snake and pointing his sword towards the nozzle where a wick ought to go. There was a hole in the top of the lamp to put oil in, between the figure of the man and the serpent.

'It's St George,' said Paul, 'what is he doing on a lamp – it ought to be Aladdin.'

Diana smiled and took the lamp gently from his hand, looking at it closely.

'Actually it's St Michael, there are differences between him and St George. Michael is another character who has had lots of names and jobs over the years. He started off as the sun god and became a Christian saint later on, but he was an archangel rather than an historic figure like St George. Look,' she said, pointing at the lamp, 'St Michael carries a sword and tackles his adversary on foot while St George rides a horse and spikes his dragon with a spear.

St George is shown actually killing the dragon whereas St Michael is usually standing over his foe, who is sometimes a demon or a dragon threatening him, but not killing him. St Michael represents light balancing the dark, not destroying it. A different situation altogether, and one which my family has been tied up with for many a long year. This figure of St Michael looks familiar, I think there is one like it in the church. Anyway finding this shows that a fraction of my dream was true. I am sure I did not know this was up the chimney since my grandfather's day. Do you think it is a clue?' she said, carefully setting the lamp on the table.

'It looks like one. Did it say something about St Michael on that old parchment? If St Michael is a light person is there anything to do with him on the map that tied in with your silver web' Paul asked, pouring over the spread map.

'Well Micklehampton is really a contraction of Michaelhampton and the church here is St Michael's, then up on Brent Tor over on the West side of the moor which I think lines up with St Michael's Mount off the coast near Penzance, is another Michael church. Our St Michael is on that line too, I would imagine. Certainly it seemed to be one of the bright lines in my dream of silver threads over the countryside so it is a good place to start from. There is no service this afternoon as Mr Pomeroy has gone to one of his other churches. I don't expect the place will be locked up at this time of day. Would you like to walk down to the village and see if we can make any sense of the clue or would you rather take Clover for a run on the moor?'

'Can't we do both?' asked Paul, 'I don't suppose it will take long to see the church and I haven't been out on the moor on foot though Dad has driven us down to Two Bridges and across to Lydford when we were looking for a house.'

'Very well,' Diana agreed, 'I will take the van down to the village with Clover in the back, then we can go out towards Widecombe and give the dog a run. I can also look for some whortleberries for jam, they grow all over the moor.'

Very soon Paul and Diana had got into the rather ancient blue van which lived in a shed the other side of the cottage, with Clover on her lead in the back. They drove through the village and up the hill to St Michael in the Moor. The old granite church with its squat tower stood at the top of a hill, almost buried in trees, dark yews and tall sycamores. It looked very like an old man hunched in a grey coat against the wind and rain among its mound of lighter and darker greenery. There was a stone wall around the churchyard which encircled the place completely except for a narrow arched gate with a roof on the side nearest the road and narrow stile on the far side. In the graveyard were dozens of ancient stones, leaning in all directions, some so old that the writing on their faces had long since been washed away into indecipherable dents and grooves by generations of moorland rain. Many of them were in the form of crosses with circles through the arms. Diana explained to Paul that the circular churchyard was an indication of the age of the holy place, now crowned with a church. In past times places of religion or healing or magic even were round and there may have been a circle of standing stones, or at least one special one at such a place. Perhaps it was still here among the monuments to long dead villagers, or had been built into the fabric of the church itself.

Up the short path they went to the pointed arch of the door, a great oaken structure with huge black iron hinges and a handle made of dark metal bent into a ring. Diana twisted it and gave a push so that the door swung inward, allowing them to pass into a small dark hallway. Beyond that a couple of paces in was another similar door which opened with a slight groan to give onto the dimly lit church beyond. It was very quiet and the strange smell of old hymn books, wilting flowers and history filled their nostrils and evoked memories of other such places.

The afternoon sun shone through panes of stained glass spreading rainbow colours onto the smooth, pale stone of the floor, and reflecting here and there onto the white walls in reds and blues and greens of strange intensity. Slowly they wandered around, Diana pointing out things of interest to Paul, the pew end carved with St Michael and opposite a fine dragon curled round on itself, watching across the nave. The intricate scroll and strap work like woven ropes was carved into the hard stone of the font. The memorial windows showing glowing saints and biblical figures bigger than life, in all sorts of brilliant coloured robes and surrounded by flowers and trees in incandescent colours. Above the altar which was rather plain there was a great figure of Michael standing over a grim looking demon, one foot on his neck and his great sword with a blade like a flame of golden glass raised to strike. His wings were brilliant pale glass which even after noon shone with reflected light all shades of yellow, gold and flame so that he sparkled and almost seemed to hover above the darker figure below. His face was hidden by his left hand which seemed to shade his eyes from the vision of evil at his feet.

'One thing about him,' said Paul, after examining the brilliant colours and spectacular play of light through the glass, 'he isn't the same as the one on your lamp as he is just pointing up. What do we do now?'

'I am sure I have seen a similar picture or carving of Michael here somewhere so we will have one last look round, then I can show you some of my ancestors, if you are interested.' Diana remarked.

Circling the small church again, examining carved pews, the roof bosses, monuments and memorials to local worthies set into the walls showed no image to match Diana's lamp so they gave up searching the inside of the church. Walking through the church yard Diana pointed out the part of the cemetery where her own family were laid to rest. Her parents had a simple cross and circle which she told Paul had been copied from a wheel cross in Cornwall near where they had spent many happy holidays. Other memorial stones had Dymond names and diamond shapes carved on them.

David, Douglas, Derek, her father, Daniel, Donald and some of the ladies of the family, Daisy, Daphne, Deborah, Dorothy and wives of the D men included Rose, Ida, Emily and Susan. Many of the names were repeated for as she had said when they first met, her family had been in the area for hundreds of years.

Walking back towards the lych gate Paul looked up at the tower. A crow stood on the edge croaking then flew downwards to land under a tree. As Paul followed its flight he noticed something carved high up on the outside of the tower.

'Look,' he called to Diana, who was intent on one of her ancestors' gravestones, 'is that a carving up there?'

Diana peered upwards and then walked to the corner of the church to get a closer view. 'It seems to me just what we are looking for. I will see if my bird watching binoculars are in the van.'

Soon she was back with a fine pair of binoculars and Clover on a short lead.

'Hang onto Clover whilst I have a look. She wouldn't let me go without her, confounded animal. Yes, you are right, it is St Michael and he is pointing towards the west. Have a look yourself.'

She took Clover's lead and gave Paul the glasses. There, high above the door to the church, on one of the corner slabs of the tower was the saint's figure. The carving was blurred with age and a frond of some plant growing out of a crevice in the stone hung down his back, but the outstretched sword was clear, as was the serpent coiling beneath his feet. He pointed westwards, over the straggling village houses to the distant tors now fading greenish purple in the afternoon sun.

'When I see Mr Pomeroy again I will ask him about that carving and see if he will let me go up to the tower. I believe there is a trapdoor above the belfry. From up there one could see exactly what he is pointing at.' Diana explained. 'Anyway, we can go up onto the moor and let Clover have a run.'

Back in the van it didn't take long to get away from the houses and following a winding narrow lane bordered with steep stone banks topped with high hedges, it was hard to see what was beyond the sides of the green tunnel they drove through. Coming round a tight bend Diana had to brake hard as a very large but thin and uncared for dog was in the middle of the road, trying to eat some poor squashed creature. It limped to one side of the road but clearly wanted to get back to its food very urgently.

'Poor thing, it doesn't look as if it had been fed for ages, and it was carrying an injured paw too.' said Diana, watching it in her driving mirror. Here the lane was covered with mud and the verges were untrimmed and shaggy. The neat hedges gave way to sagging and rusty barbed wire and the stones of the walls were tumbled into the road as if livestock had escaped over the feeble fences. A wide farm gateway between rotting wooden fences came into view. Again, there was mud and rubbish all over the roadway and a sagging notice, badly painted on a bit of broken board read Grimpen Farm PRIVATE KEEP OUT.

'What a miserable place,' said Paul as they drove by, 'it looks as if no-one has taken any care with it, like that dog. I bet it lives there and no-one cares about anything, not even keeping the fences mended.'

'It is a horrible place,' replied Diana, 'it is always coming up before the local council for breaking by-laws or something. Mr Nigel Blytes who owns the place is mainly a battery chicken farmer with thousands of birds in tiny cages having nothing to do all day but eat and lay eggs. That's a vile existence to wish on any creature. He is only concerned with profits and does nothing to the rest of his land except rent the fields out to anyone for grazing at high rents. He expects his tenants to mend his fences and blames them if their cattle stray. The grass is poor because it has had no attention for years and has been over-grazed so the cattle get sick and then make it worse. It is a shocking state of affairs and no-one gets on with him or his horrid labourers. They are sometimes down in the Green Man, drinking too much and starting fights with the villagers. They get high wages and boast to the other farm labourers but the local lads have feelings for their livestock and money is no compensation for cruelty.' Diana was showing her anger at the thought of the place as they drove away from Grimpen Farm and out onto the high, clean moors.

Parking on a patch of gravel at the side of a road with no hedges or fences, not far from the slatted cattle grids which prevent animals getting off the moorland grazing, because they can't balance on the narrow rails, Diana let Clover out of the back of the van. She took a plastic box for whortleberries and soon she and Paul were striding down the hillside towards a trickling brook where low growing bushes with pale greenish leaves, now beginning to colour rust and russet grew in profusion. Clover almost vanished among the patches of bracken except that the waving white plumed tail showed her whereabouts. Diana stopped and showed Paul the small dark misted bluish-purple berries lurking like gems under the leaves. Gradually the box began to fill and the sun sank towards the distant dark hills. Clover raced to and fro then after a long drink from the clear stream she nosed up to her mistress, showing she had had enough exercise and thought it was time to go home. Diana consulted her watch and told Paul that it was after five. Soon they were trundling back over the cattle grid, heading back towards the village with a box full of fresh whortleberries for Diana to cook. Paul's head was buzzing with all sorts of ideas about the open countryside and its associations with St Michael.

Diana broke into his train of thoughts 'Tomorrow I will go into Exeter and get some larger scale maps of this area and try to mark the silver strands I saw in my dreams. I can't really go writing all over the new map and we may have to go out and explore places if we are to find these ancient Hallows on the moor.' Soon they came back into the village. She stopped at the end of the lane leading to Paul's house. 'Please thank your mother for the bone for Clover. If

I find anything of interest I will let you know. Don't lose any sleep over this puzzle as you might need your wits to help me sort out this strange quest. I must say, in the few days since you fell at my feet I have got further in this search than for years before. Thanks for your help.' She smiled as Paul got out of the van and drove away with all sorts of ideas swarming in her mind.

'Well, I must say that Mrs Dymond makes sure you get back in time for meals,' said Paul's mother as he came through the door, 'did you have a good afternoon? Your Dad finished the roses and we had a bonfire with the bits. The garden will look grand next summer at this rate. Wash your hands and then bring in this plate of bread and butter. There is a cherry cake on the table and some jam and paste as I bet you are hungry. After tea I want to pick your brains on a holiday competition. We could win a winter trip to the sun.'

Chapter Six
Reward and Discovery

After the tea things had been washed up and put away Paul's mother spread out a colourful brochure on the table.

'This is a place called Villa da Luz in Portugal, it is a holiday village by the sea and it is so warm you can pick oranges off the trees in January. Look at those little white houses in among gardens and all covered with flowering creepers and palms and whatnot. There are some orange and lemon groves and almond trees in flower in winter. If you can write a slogan and send in some wrappers from Portuguese fruit you can win a family holiday in the New Year there by the sea with lots of food and grapes for wine which they grow there, firework shows and nightly discos, dances and music. It sounds fantastic.' Paul examined the pictures of the exotic food and tropical looking beach scenes and saw the verse which began "Portugal, a place for fun......" The competition asked people to list certain things in order of their choice and finish the verse. His mother had filled in the squares with her selection of choices but was obviously stuck with the poem. Paul thought for a moment or two and then said 'What about Portugal, a place for fun, for fruit and fish and lots of sun!' His mother and father considered for a while and agreed it sounded reasonable and with no further ado completed the competition form and his mother put it into an envelope ready to post in the morning.

'You better have a bath and then bed if you've got school tomorrow' said his Dad, looking at the TV programmes in the paper. 'Did you finish that tree project?'

Paul said that he had and that his notes and very wilted leaves were in a plastic carrier bag with his books to take to school next day. Soon he as in bed without having to perform the spell to make him dream but dream he did of warm sea and red sandy cliffs and orange trees and fishing boats with eyes painted on their prows filled with shining silver fish trapped in a silver net which was somehow spread out over the countryside, a darker, greener, more familiar land. There were holes in the net and Paul woke up wondering if the light would get out through the holes but he could hear his mother's alarm clock ringing and sunlight streamed onto the walls of his room.

At school he presented his project and Mr Larkin seemed quite pleased. When the lesson ended his teacher called him up to his desk.

'You have done very well for a newcomer Paul, in fact your work is a lot better than some of these local lads who ought to know every plant on the moor. You did all this work yourself didn't you?'

'Oh, yes, I did,' replied Paul, swallowing hard, 'I borrowed a book on trees from Diana Dymond as I was picking the branches from her hedge. She didn't help me though, only to check that I had found all the trees in her book. I did all the drawings and copied the information myself.'

'Good, it was a fine attempt at something which must be a bit difficult at first. How do you like this country area?' enquired his teacher sounding extremely friendly.

'I am just beginning to get used to the size and emptiness. I went up onto the moor yesterday and helped pick whortleberries. There wasn't a building or other manmade thing in sight. It seemed quite empty and unlived in. Very different from London.'

'It used to be quite populated round here long ago,' said Mr

Larkin, 'in fact I thought you might like a treat. If you can tear yourself away from the football on Wednesday afternoon you could join my other class for a trip to one of the ancient villages on the moor, if your parents will let you come. Here is a note for them to sign if you would like that.'

'That would be smashing,' replied Paul enthusiastically, 'there is something about this place that has got a hold on me. It is full of strange things and people. Bits of London are old and there are heaps of museums but down here history is all over the place, you almost begin to expect to see the odd druid pottering about in the village or some Roman soldiers making camp. I don't know what it is, it's like Dr Who and Time being different or something... I think I can manage without football for once, I played a lot in London. We had plastic turf on one pitch so it never got muddy or cut up. Shall I give you this back tomorrow if my Mum will sign it?'

'Yes, I will be in the hall after register so you can let me know then.' Mr Larkin left him alone.

Paul set off to the dining hall to see what today presented, fresh fish out of the sea or oranges, or there might be macaroni cheese and syrup pudding which he liked. He found he was wrong on both counts, it was what the boys called snake and sydney pie and traffic jam tart. Anyway, Daniel Whiddon knew how to feed starving youngsters.

When he got home he quickly did his maths homework before his mother came in and while she was in a good mood preparing a salad for tea he explained about the special outing and gave her the note from Mr Larkin. It was headed "Afternoon visit to Great Dog Tor and Moorland Ancient Hut Circles" and explained that Mr Larkin was taking a small group of students to look at the sites on the moor. Boys and girls were advised to bring a waterproof and wear stout shoes as these would be quite a bit of walking. A snack would also be essential as it was a remote place with no facilities.

Parents agreeing to allow their child to join the party should sign on the dotted line.

Paul's mother looked at him, 'You're doing all right at school then, getting asked to join special outings. You better keep it up and come Christmas we might be able to arrange a surprise for you. Here you are, I've signed the form. Go and eat your tea and then you can watch the telly.'

Paul was tucking into his plate of salad, much of which has been grown in the village, when he heard his father's voice outside the door and another familiar voice answering.

'Come on in then if you have time for a cup of tea no doubt Mary can spare you one. Look who I've found down in the village shop.' Paul's Dad came into the kitchen closely followed by Diana.

'Hello dear,' said Paul's Mum, bringing another cup and plate to the table, 'I hope this lad of mine isn't bothering you or stopping you getting on with things. He is a great one for chattering when you want to finish a bit of work. By the way, I'm Mary and this is George, the Sparrow bit you know from Paul I expect. Have you got time for tea?' Diana seemed pleased to be invited.

Soon they were all eating ham and lettuce, tomatoes and spring onions and then going onto cherry cake which was one of Paul's Mum's specialities. Diana began telling Paul's parents about her family and the quest for the lost treasures as she then called the Hallows. She managed to make it sound respectable, almost ordinary, to be hunting for strange and wondrous things by mentioning archaeological digs and historical surveys. She explained that her father had sought the ancient hiding places of the Hallows as had her grandfather and many of the Dymonds before him. She also said how much Paul was helping her, his recent arrival and different outlook was giving her a new angle on some of the old problems of the quest and she did hope, with Paul's assistance, to have discovered something by Christmas. Diana said she hoped Paul's mother wouldn't mind if Paul came out on the moor sometimes or perhaps helped her studying old maps or even digging around particular sites if it became necessary. Somehow Diana managed to give the impression that Paul was doing a valuable job and ought to be encouraged. Certainly she didn't mention magic nor strange dreams caused by herbal pillows being part of her system of investigation. It ended up with Paul's parents both encouraging him to help her all he could and as she went home they assured her that, school and homework permitting, Paul was welcome to spend his time with Diana until he became a nuisance or she had no need of his help.

'What a charming person,' said Paul's Dad as the door closed behind Diana, 'she sounds so interesting with all her talk about local customs and history. I am sure Paul will learn a lot about this part of the world in her company. Oh, by the way, she gave me this note in the shop to give you before I persuaded her to come to tea. She was going to drop it in on her way home.'

Paul took the envelope on which his name was written in artistic twirly letters and on turning it over discovered a blob of gold sealing wax and the diamond D impressed into it. Paul opening it along the top so as not to spoil the seal for he had never had such a letter before. His eyes lit up as he read "To my friend and companion on the quest, this news. I have located the maps of the area and will trace upon them the lines which I described to you. When this is done, perhaps you may spare an hour or so to ponder them and see if it is indeed another clue! Under the wings of St Michael, Diana."

He explained what was in the letter to his Dad who was trying to watch a quiz programme on the TV, and asked if he could go and look at the maps soon

'Not tonight, my lad, as it is dark now but if you get your homework done early tomorrow you can go to the Rowans for a while if Miss Dymond is in.' and he turned his concentration back to the man on the box who was trying to explain the meaning of "pyramidology" in less than 30 seconds.

The next day at school Paul gave Mr Larkin the note about the outing, suffered through a French lesson, an art class and history which was concerned with trade in the middle ages. He enjoyed his macaroni cheese for lunch and in the afternoon English lesson found his mind straying to Diana's letter and wondering if she had written it with a quill pen. His teacher saw his inattention and asked Paul what he was thinking about. Paul said a friend had sent him a strange, old fashioned letter for a joke. His teacher said it would be a good subject for homework, to write a letter from one of the characters in the book they were studying to another, using proper language, and if anyone felt artistic they could try using a steel nibbed pen instead of a biro and do italic writing. He then ignored the book which Paul thought was boring and showed them how to write old fashioned lettering. Paul was quite pleased at this as he could properly ask Diana about her letter and perhaps borrow her seal to make it look old, anyway if was a bit more interesting than having to write three sides on the importance of one character in a story which he had seen as a film. He was very pleased to hear the bell ring for the end of the day and was off home as fast as he could go with his bag of books bumping his shoulder as he ran.

It didn't take him very long to grab a piece of bread and jam, swig from the bottle of milk and scribble a note to tell his mother where he had gone before he was off down the road to the Rowans.

Clover barked as he knocked on the cottage door and Diana opened it with her hands covered with red juice and a trickle of the same down her white jersey.

'Come in and shut the door, I am just straining the elderberry juice into the fermentation bottles. Can you fetch that small saucepan off the Aga for me, it has the sterilised cork for this jar. It is much easier to get them to fit tightly if they are warm.'

She took a red rubber bung and a fancy glass tube with bends and bubbles blown in its stem and carefully inserted it into the top of a large glass jar full of deep crimson juice. She stood it on a shelf in the alcove near the stove and soon the water in the bend of the tube was being pushed sideways and a loud glub issued from the bottle.

'That will ferment until all the sugar has been converted and the juice has become quite a strong, dry wine.' she explained to Paul as she rinsed her hands. 'I will bottle it then. Anyway, come into the other room and we can have a look at the map. It might give us a clue where to look for these Hallows or your genius might suggest something I haven't thought of.'

Diana had bought the large scale maps of the area and carefully stuck them together to make a huge sheet covering about a quarter of the moor and all the lanes and cottages around the village. Paul soon located his own home and Rowans which was named on the map. Here and there Diana had drawn fine lines with a pencil, scarcely marking the paper. They seemed to fan out in both directions making a sort of X shape with something in the village as the crossing point. On looking closer Paul saw that it was the symbol for a church with a tower ⊠ so it must be St Michael in the Moor. Diana had also drawn tiny circles round marks on the map where old fashioned letters said "standing stone" or "stone circle", "round barrow" or "stone row". These seemed to run in straight lines too, a most strange arrangement for such old things. Diana explained she had done some reading in Exeter library and found that research had been done on the alignments of ancient sites and that there were lines called "leys" which joined many of them in straight lines. If was not certain whether the ley was a line of some sort of natural earth power which the ancient people could detect and so place their stones, barrows or circles upon them, or if by building a number of constructions in a straight line, surveyed from site to site by lighting beacon fires at night, that a line of some sort of power was formed. In China apparently such alignments were called "Feng Shui" or dragon paths and many of the lines in Britain had dragons carved in churches, churches dedicated either to St Michael or St George, both long associated with dragons or other local tales of great worms or serpents. It was possible, according to the books she had read, to discover the ley lines themselves by dowsing or divining for them with a pendulum. You could try a dowsing rod, like the ones used to find water, made for preference from a hazel twig or modern ones made out of a pair of wire coat hangers cut and bent into L shapes that sit in some sort of handles too. When someone crossed over a ley line the rod or pendulum would react strongly in a certain way and show where it was. Some people could even find the lines on a map without having to trek about in wet fields or boggy moorlands. Diana said that these lines ran between such things as cairns of stones, burial mounds, standing single or groups or circles of stones, embankments, pools of water in hollows and notches cut into the skyline. Some of these lines had become paths and it may have been such straight routes which were later paved and became roman roads in some places. Judging by the dozens of ancient constructions all over Dartmoor there must be heaps of ley lines which seemed to be the strands of the silver web she had seen in her dream.

As well as the light spots there were the dark places where the land was spoiled, the wells polluted and the fields made barren which had shown up black in the pattern. Perhaps if some of the Hallows were found these murky places could be brightened up and the whole pattern restored.

'What we need is a plan,' said Diana firmly, 'it would be hopeless trying to explore the moor inch by inch, and anyway there are bogs and mires out there where whole herds of ponies have vanished without trace. Watch out for the greenest bits, if you go out there, they are very dangerous. There were supposed to be thirteen treasures which gives us lots of things to hunt for. According to various Welsh bards these Hallows included a sword and whetstone, a mantle, a horse's bridle, the Grail, a basket, a drinking horn, a chariot, a platter, a robe, a chessboard, a knife and a cooking pot. Different authors give slight variations but those are the most likely translations for the objects. Obviously many of them, if there were an actual set, would have rotted away, although museums do have examples of old cloth and woven basketwork which have been preserved. Also, these things have the reputation of changing their form so perhaps they still exist as something else. Not a great deal of help to us now though.'

'Still,' cut in Paul, 'if it is possible to find them by following a dragons flight path or something you ought to recognise them when we get there. Will there be a rainbow do you think, 'cos they say there is gold at the end of the rainbow? Let's have another look at that map and see if it gives any more clues. Haven't you got a spell for discovering all these Hallows in one go?'

Diana shook her head, 'As I said before, you can't just find them like that or a good witch or magician long ago would have found them. It requires more than skill, cunning and intelligence. It is a sort of initiative test so that whoever does find them is bright enough to make use of them. One other thing I discovered in the library was that the line which goes from St Michael's Mount in Cornwall to Bury St Edmunds in Norfolk is on a line with the sunrise on May Day. Apparently that is thought to be one of the ways in which the very long lines were set so straight by having watchers on every hilltop before dawn on a special day and as the sun rose they set up markers to point to the exact spot on the horizon where the sun appeared. Later on, stones or cairns or notches were made to mark the line. Clever people our ancestors, a lot more so than they are usually given credit for, woad daubed barbarians indeed!'

'If you are right then, if we follow one of the lines you saw we ought to come to a place where the Hallows are hidden or at least some of them. St Michael is supposed to point out the route so what do you suggest we do? Did you draw the line the carving was pointing along or wasn't that one you saw?'

Diana showed him the map and there were parts of the line but it ran right through the farm marked "Grimpen" and there were no obvious stones or circles shown along it beyond the farmhouse. The only mark on the map was the track of a footpath leading towards a wood and a small tor of rocks called Gablestone Tor. Apart from deciding to have a walk along the path sometime to see if there was anything to be discovered there didn't seem any further ideas to be considered. Paul then explained about the homework letter and asked if Diana would show him how she had produced the seal and the old fashioned writing so that he could make another effort for his teacher. They did try to make school work interesting. No-one in Hoxton went on outings to anything more exciting than a local museum or mouldering old building.

Diana rummaged in her cupboard again and brought out a packet of paper which looked at first like parchment, a bottle of brown ink and a pen holder of chewed red wood with a broad steel nib. She apologised for not having a goose quill but said she would look out for some big feathers if she walked across one of the turkey farms in the district. Dipping the wide nib into the ink Diana showed Paul the rather awkward style of holding the pen so that it made thick and thin lines. Soon he could manage letters of the alphabet and so she offered to lend him the things for his homework. She also dug about in a cupboard and found a different seal, one with a carving of Britannia cut into what looked like hard, purple glass, and a stick of sealing wax.

'Wet the seal with something then press it into the warm wax before it sets and you will get a clear impression,' she explained to Paul as he gathered the pen, ink, paper, seal and wax into a small box.

'Is it tomorrow you go out for your walk on the moor with your school?' Diana asked as he walked through the kitchen where Clover pounced on him, bounding about and trying to reach up and lick his hands.

'Yes, I am!' said Paul

'Come on Clover, I will walk into the village to give you a bit of a run as you were shut in whilst I was in Exeter this morning.' Diana took her collar and lead from its peg and buckled the collar round her neck so they followed Paul into the garden. 'Would your mother like some vegetables do you think?' Diana asked, trying to hold Clover who was eager to be off for a run, 'There are some marrows under the hedge and I think the cauliflowers towards the flower garden are about ready for cutting. There are lots of lettuce too, if you like 'cos, you know the long thin ones.'

'Anything you can spare would be all right,' Paul replied, 'Mum does a super cauliflower cheese and we often have salad while the weather is still warm.'

Diana returned to the cottage, giving Clover's lead to Paul, and soon returned with a knife and a carrier bag. Together they explored the neat rows of plants and Diana soon found a large cauliflower, still enveloped in its dark green leaves. She also searched about under the wide green foliage of the marrow plant to select a suitable sized marrow, dark green and striped with yellow. Tapping it gently with the handle of her knife to see if it was hollow sounding and so really ripe, she cut the stalk and gave it to Paul. Towards the corner of the garden was a patch of pale green lettuce, both round and long ones, with spaces where some of their number had already been sacrificed to the table. When she had cut several of them Diana sliced off the muddy roots and taking the stalk of the cauliflower she had cut for Paul, she flung them towards the compost heap at the bottom of the hedge. Without thinking she also threw the knife and they both heard it strike against a stone in the wall.

'Sit, Clover,' Diana commanded, 'you are not to go off retrieving sharp knives. Stay...'

Both she and Paul went to search along the stone bank to

recover the kitchen knife. Obviously it had fallen against the bank but the long grass and weeds hid it completely. They both peered among the greenery, Paul scrambling up the bank itself, to see if it had lodged among the hedgerow trees. One of his feet slipped as he climbed and he was about to repeat his tumble which had introduced him to Diana when his foot caught on another stone. From it he leapt down to the narrow path which edged the vegetable plot. A small avalanche of stones and weeds followed and the thump he made landing made Diana look up.

'Hey,' she cried, her voice full of excitement, 'look at that!'

Where Paul had brought down the tumble of stones and weeds there was now a single slab of granite, its surface pale and glittering with mica. Into the face which was now clearer was a much eroded but none the less still readable letter D.

'Well, I never' she exclaimed, 'I have played in this garden since I was an infant, yet I never discovered that carved stone. It must be a part of the quest I am sure.'

'Can you dig it out, get a lever or something and see if there is one of the Hallows underneath.' said Paul, trying to pull away more of the grass and small stones around the granite boulder.

'Well, I don't think I can shift it on my own and it is beginning to get late now. Tomorrow I will have another look at it and see if it can be moved. I will be able to clear away some more of this undergrowth to see the rest of the bank. I don't want my garden hedge to come down now, do I?'

'Can I help then, it won't matter if I miss school for one day I'm sure. It is far more important to find your treasures.' Paul added, with desperation in his voice.

'Oh you can't go missing school, especially not tomorrow with your trip to the old village that you earned for good work. I will tell you what though. I promise not to tell anyone else about our discovery and if I can't shift the stone on my own I will wait until you can come and help. Does that satisfy you?'

Paul looked glum but agreed, after all, it was Diana's own hedge and her quest so he couldn't dictate what she ought to do. Anyway, it was past his supper time and he was hungry, also he still had his letter to do for homework so with Diana and Clover at his heels he set off smartly for home. He was very excited at their new discovery but decided that if Diana was not going to tell anyone about the finding of the engraved stone he wouldn't mention it either. He made a vow of silence but inside he was bubbling over with the lucky throw which had led to the discovery, and tomorrow Diana might uncover some part of her special inheritance.

Chapter Seven
Moorland Mysteries

Paul's mother was very pleased with the fresh vegetables straight from Diana's garden and promised to cook them the following day but a dish of sausages and mash was waiting in the oven and Paul was more than ready to tuck in as soon as he had washed his hands. There was some stewed fruit for pudding and when that was out of the way Paul had to get on with his letter for homework. He found that the steel nib made his not very neat handwriting much more readable and the brown ink looked really old. He hadn't any good ideas about what the Dickensian characters might have written to each other about so it was not a long letter. Still, he managed a nice print of the seal, even if it did come out upside down, by accident. When he had added a flourishing signature he began to yawn and soon climbed into bed. No-one had asked him what he had been doing all evening so he had no reason to talk about Diana's new clue to her quest. He went to sleep wondering about shining stones and carved letters.

Next morning he was up early. His mother was making sandwiches to take on his trip to the moorland village. He also collected a pair of wellingtons that his mother had bought when they first moved west but which he hadn't actually worn, and a bright orange cagoule with a hood and lots of pockets in case it rained. With these things and his homework letter safe in his bag he set off down the lane.

During the morning he found it hard to concentrate on maths and he was glad the geography lesson was nearly all a matter of looking at some slides of how rubber and coconuts were grown and harvested and turned into useful things. At lunchtime he soon ate his chicken pie and peas and lemon sponge and custard and went off to join the bunch of youngsters who were clustering round the school's white minibus. Soon Mr Larkin arrived with a list in his hand and called out the names of the twelve children who were making the trip with him. Paul turned to one of the others and asked where all the rest of the class of 30 or so were.

'They're all staying in school to see a film about life in an ancient village reconstructed by some archaeologists. Only us few wanted to go out on the moor, most of us have lived here all our lives and know the places quite well. I like it out there because of the animals and birds.' said the other lad.

Soon they had climbed aboard the bus and were off into the cloudy afternoon light. It wasn't long before they turned off the main road onto a twisting unfenced lane, bumped over a cattle grid and trundled up among the rolling green hills of the moors. In the distance they caught glimpses of tumbled rocky tors sticking out, grey about the green and purple of the heather and rough grass. After about twenty minutes the van turned into a large car parking area and stopped, facing across the empty space to the piled rocks of Great Dog Tor. Mr Larkin turned to the boys and girls in the bus and began to explain what was going to happen. He wanted them to divide into four groups of three, each of whom would be given a question sheet. Working as a team they were to find answers to the questions and write the answers in the spaces on the sheet.

The children were to stay within view of the Tor and come back at once when he tooted the horn three times as it would then be four o'clock and time to go home. Because Paul was new to the area he was partnered with Pete, a tall dark boy a year older than himself, and Susan who had curly fair hair and was smartly dressed in a school skirt, long white socks and shiny lace-up shoes. Her jumper looked new and she looked by far the most tidy of the bunch of children as they set off across the grass towards the rocks.

Mr Larkin led them all over the edge of the first tor and down the hollow beyond. There they were shown the round walls of huts which had been built in the Bronze Age, about 4,000 years ago. Some of the walls, built of unshaped stones, yet fitted so well together that they still stood up to the level of the waists of the youngsters, made almost complete circles, others were little more than hummocks of turf grown over ragged piles of tumbled stone. Some huts stood alone, others nestled close to each other, as if for warmth or protection from the ever blowing moorland wind. Here and there were niches which might have been cupboards, or stones with hollows to support posts which held up the thatched roofs. In some huts the remains of hearths were still visible, also hollowed stones with small pools of water from recent rains reflected the clouds scudding across the sky. It was interesting to imagine the ancient people with their family and animals squatting round these same fireplaces so long ago and watching the same sun set over the same, unchanged hills.

'So different from London,' thought Paul, 'for that has been changed by people every few years, putting up tall flats or knocking them down again.'

Mr Larkin called them all together and handed out the boards with the question sheets clipped to them to each of the groups.

'Now look here you lot, don't go getting lost or damage these old walls. If it starts to rain or gets misty come at once back to the bus with your group. I know I can trust you all to be sensible and do those question sheets without my having to stand all the time watching you but I don't want any of you lost either. Do you understand? When you finish, come back to the bus. The canteen ladies have sent a big flask of tea and some buns for you. Now get on with you and I don't want the Yell Hounds following you back to school either!' With that, he turned to walk back over the Tor to the bus to sit in the sun and wait for the children to do their work sheets.

'What's the Yell Hound?' asked Paul as soon as Mr Larkin had gone. Susan looked blank and muttered something about old tales but Pete, whose accent sounded very Devon, said they were the hounds of the Wild Hunt, the Gabriel Hounds, which could be heard hunting evil doers across the moors on any stormy night. They were white hounds, as big as Alsatians, with red ears and eyes which glowed with fire in the darkness and the huntsman was a great horned and winged being who followed them on a white horse through the skies. The noise of them baying got louder the further away they were and when they were really close you could scarcely hear them at all. Nothing was safe from them and animals and men would be chased until they were caught or dropped with exhaustion. Susan looked very pale and kept trying to interrupt what Pete was saying. Paul was delighted, it was almost as good as the things that Diana said. 'Is that true?' he asked, 'Do they really chase across here or is it just a story?'

'This moor is very strange,' continued Pete, who was very fond of weird tales, 'there's lots of ghosts up here and folk vanishing into the mires and never being seen again. There are old villages with graveyards the other side of the moor and the funeral processions still go on as spooks, hundreds of years after they started. You want to hear my old Dad going on about this place. He'd scare the boots off you.'

'What about these questions, then,' said Susan, at last finding something to get the talk away from things which frightened her, 'It says "Draw the plan of the biggest hut and describe its most important feature."'

Paul was sure he had already looked into that hut and it still had a fireplace and a sort of bench of stones along one side. The others decided that must be right and Pete filled in the space. The next question was "Where do you think the people got their water from?" There was no stream immediately by the village of hut circles so they began to walk away a bit, down the hill.

'What else do we have to find out?' asked Paul. 'We may have to go somewhere else and we don't want to have to spend ages wandering all over this moor, it must go on for miles.'

'There are only four questions,' answered Susan, who was still carrying the board. 'The next is "What else can you see which might have been the work of the Bronze Age people?" and the last one is "What kind of animals do you think these people had and how did they look after them?" It doesn't help much as they could have done all sorts of things like planting heather in their gardens which is still growing here, or making things that we don't know about.' Susan went on, sounding a bit fed up already.

'Don't you be so daft, Su,' said Pete, 'they didn't have flower gardens to grow heather in though the sheep here graze on it when it has been swaled, that is, burnt off. I reckon they would have kept sheep, ponies, cows and pigs and probably had dogs to herd 'em with, so put that down under the animals question. I 'spect they would have let them graze all over the moor as the farmers still do, and rounded them up once a year for sorting out. The best ones would be kept in pens through the winter and the rest killed and salted down to feed the people, I reckon.'

'What about their cats and rabbits as pets?' said Susan, who didn't seem to understand history at all.

'I didn't think there were rabbits in England till later on,' said Paul. 'In London in history we did a thing about what animals came in when. I can't remember if it was the Romans or the Normans who brought in rabbits but they weren't here in the Bronze Age. I don't know about cats though.'

For a while they discussed the answers but were still left with the water question and the one about other works of Bronze Age people.

'Perhaps they used rain water and didn't wash much,' said Susan, 'or damned up streams in the winter to make pools for the summer.' It didn't seem to be quite right but neither Paul nor Pete could think of anything better and let Susan fill in that space.

'Do you think he means things like standing stones or circles and things?' queried Paul, trying to remember what Diana had said about ancient remains. 'On the map of the moor are all sorts of mounds and barrows which are supposed to be ancient, does Larky mean them?'

'The question is "What can you see..." so we will have to look for something like that. I think we can go up that next ridge where those rocks are and see if there are any obvious standing stones, not these piles of old rubble, or anything like walls for sheep pens or anything like that.' said Pete, striding off up the other side of the valley, away from the village. Susan followed protesting about her socks getting dirty from the long grass and her legs getting prickled from the tough heather stems and whortleberry plants. Paul strolled along, enjoying the feeling of space and air, the rolling green and purple hills, as far as their eye could see. No factory chimneys, no tall manmade buildings cluttered the view, no decaying old houses blotted out the light. He watched the skyline and began to notice its sharp outline was fading a bit, becoming fuzzy or clouded, but he paid little attention.

Susan was picking sprays of heather and the leaves of the whortleberries which were beginning to turn autumn shades of russet and orange. She suddenly began to run forward, down the next slope where the grass grew deep and green, lush as a summer lawn and here and there dotted with bobbing white plumes, like small bundles of fur on slender stems. She bent to pick these dabs of white, rushing onwards towards the bobbing specks which seemed to grow more profusely always a bit further out of reach. Soon, she was quite a distance away and she gave a sudden frightened yell 'Help, I'm sinking, it's a bog.' Wildly she struggled, trying desperately to pull her feet from the squelchy mud and pools of water which surrounded her. The harder she struggled the worse it became until she was over her ankles among the bright green grass with its nodding, tempting plumes of marsh cotton grass. Pete stood still, his mouth open but he could think of nothing to shout. Paul knew nothing of the deadly mires except what Diana had said and she hadn't explained how to get out of one. 'Stay still.' yelled Pete at last, having collected his scattered wits, 'The more you thrash about the deeper you'll go. Rest easy and we will get you out. Somehow.' he added under his breath. Susan took no notice but carried on flinging herself about and yelling words that neither of them could make out.

She was almost down to her knees now and when Pete and Paul tried to walk towards her they started to sink in the soft mud. It was obviously a matter of getting help and doing it quickly if Susan was to be rescued before she sank altogether. Paul remembered that Diana had said that ponies had disappeared into the marshes and they were much bigger than Susan. Paul looked back up the hill down which Susan had so blithely run, picking her flowers, and saw to his dismay that the creeping low cloud which he had seen stealing silently over the other hills was now closing in.

In clammy swathes it drifted on the breeze, filling the hollow where they stood, helplessly watching Susan's plight. White streamers swirled and joined, cutting out the sun and the blue of the sky, shading the green and purple moors to mouldy grey. The grass was changing from green to grey dewed white and the warmth of the afternoon was swiftly fading to a chilly dusk. If Susan was scared she could at least scream but Paul was frightened and totally bewildered, even more so because he was completely lost in a strange place and enclosed in an uncanny mist. He might as well have been on Mars for all he knew what to do next. Pete alone had an idea what ought to be done but unless Susan would stop yelling and listen and then act as he explained there was no way in which the two boys could rescue her.

With the unexpected change in the weather, the Dartmoor mist coming down there was little chance of Larky or the other kids finding them, that is even if they bothered to look. More likely they would sit in the bus and wait for the missing team, grumbling because they were going to be late for tea and might miss favourite telly programmes. They wouldn't know that the others were struggling for their lives in a bottomless mire.

'I'm freezing!' Susan yelled, the first thing they had been able to understand for some minutes, 'Don't leave me, help me, oh please help me.' She was sobbing wildly and seemed too tired to go on struggling into the soggy pool of dark mud and water which now almost reached her waist.

'We must throw her something warm to wear.' said Pete, beginning to remember things he had been told, 'Have you got anything you can spare?'

Paul nodded and pulled the orange cagoule from his bag and Pete took off his woolly jumper, putting his jacket on again, and a rather tatty old anorak which he took from the satchel slung over his shoulder. With care they rolled each garment into a ball, tying the sleeves together so that it could be thrown across the mire. Pete shouted to Susan, warned her to catch and carefully, with a gentle under arm lob, threw his jumper to her. It just missed her spread fingers but fell close to her. By leaning sideways she caught hold of it and frantically unravelled it, pulling it on over her other clothes. Next, Pete threw Paul's cagoule but just as he was about to toss it to Susan, Paul yelled for him to stop.

'What's the matter, don't you want it to get wet?' asked Pete, puzzled.

'No, hang on a mo, there is a long piece of cord through the bottom. If you keep hold of one end you will have a line to Susan. We might be able to pass things to her or at least keep in touch if this mist closes in completely. There is another cord through the edge of the hood, pull that right out and tie the other cord to it then when you chuck it, hang on.'

Quickly they joined the two cords, leaving the shorter one still threaded through the neck. Paul tested the knot then allowed Pete to screw up the light cagoule and toss it to Susan who caught it with both hands. She struggled into its folds and had a job to get her head through the neck where the cord pulled it tight. In the end she managed and the bright orange showed her up clearly in the mist.

'Look,' said Paul, 'now we've got a line to Susan can't we find something a bit stronger and haul her out. Does the strap come off your bag?'

'I can unbuckle a bit of mine and we could join them together and perhaps pull her out.'

Pete examined his satchel but its leather strap was firmly riveted to the rest of it. Without a knife between them they couldn't cut it.

Paul took most of the strap off the sports bag which he used for school as it could be worn long or short and about 3 feet of strong plastic shoulder strap came off. When he buckled it to the long side of the leather belt on Pete's satchel it seemed to be long enough to reach to Susan.

'If we throw the satchel to her and hang onto the strap she might be able to be pulled out. Susan, listen, we are going to tie Pete's satchel to this cord for you to pull over then if you can hang on we will try to haul you out. Do you understand?'

Susan was sobbing still but she drew a grimy hand across her face and nodded, without a word. When told she began to slowly draw the cord in and the satchel slid over the wet ground, Paul keeping a firm hold onto the end of the strap. As soon as she had the leather satchel in her hands Pete began to explain to her what to do. If she could put some of her weight onto the bag and some of it on the board with the questions which would support her over the squishy surface.

At first she stayed stuck still grasping the two items to her, afraid to make any more, but after Pete's shouting and Paul's quieter encouragement, she started to lean forward onto the board and the satchel, grasping it firmly near the strap. Pete and Paul began to heave on the strap. Their feet slid on the soft marshy ground but gradually they got a firmer grip and Susan's weight spread out over the two items didn't sink so far. It was hard work and they were all tired, Susan was very frightened, not least by the thought of being pulled into another bog head first. Inch by inch she was sledged over the surface of the mire, lying flat on the board and satchel, clutching hard with both hands. As she moved she began to kick her feet free, then she tried to crawl but began to sink again. With a cry of panic she lurched forward. Pete and Paul pulled with all their might and with a horrible slurping noise she shot forward and tumbled on top of them at the edge of the bog.

For a few minutes it was chaos, Susan sobbed wildly and clutched the two boys who were shaking with tiredness and embarrassed by this show of emotion from the girl. After a bit they all calmed down and helped her scrape the worst of the mud from her legs and skirt. Paul scrubbed at her face and hands with his hanky, now more black than white, and smeared the two white patches made through the grim by tears wider. Soon they were all feeling a bit better, especially as Paul found he still had the sandwiches his mother had made and a large piece of cake which he shared among them all. Lastly there was an apple which they passed round for they were all thirsty in the clammy mist.

When they were ready to move on Pete noticed that the wind had risen and that tendrils of mist were passing by. Shapes of rocks began to appear and then the stones themselves. Soon the grass changed back from dim grey to green and the hills emerged, strange and distant as the Dartmoor wind took it away as silently and swiftly as it had appeared. It was still cloudy with patches of mist resting in hollows, clinging to damper areas, swirling and hunching itself about all over the landscape. Looking up the slope where they now found themselves Paul saw a tall, upright stone, too big to be left over from the ice age, too small and straight to be natural.

He clambered up the rise to stand beside it, hoping desperately that he would see the rugged rocks of Great Dog Tor but he was disappointed. All round were hills and valleys with similar greeny-mauve shapes, none bearing any sign of the works of man. Pete climbed up beside him and the shivering unhappy figure of Susan hunched against them, partly from cold, partly from fear.

'Which way should we go then?' asked Paul, staring at the distant horizon all around, 'Can you tell where we came from?'

Pete looked blank and Susan hid her face in her hands and her shoulders shook as tears streamed down her face. Neither she nor Pete had any idea of which way they had come, and in the mist, whilst Susan was stuck in the mire, they had circled round, seeking firmer ground on which to walk to her rescue. The sun had been hidden by clouds when they had begun their walk over the moor so even shadows didn't help, now that the sky was clearing and the sun sinking westwards. Paul stared all round then suddenly noticed something. In one direction there seemed to be a rough mound of stones, not enough to be the remains of a hut circle but definitely not just an outcrop of rock. It seemed to be perched on a small rise of ground in the valley below, to the side of the greener land of the marsh. Paul moved round behind the tall stone and looked towards the rock pile. Beyond them, the next slope climbed gently to the distant sky and there Paul saw something else. Very faintly, where the dark green touched the grey edge of the clouds was a slight dip, a narrow notch in the skyline.

Closing his eyes to cut out the glare he turned right round, searching the horizon but only in that one place, above the heap of stones was there any trace of a notch. Paul grabbed Pete's arm and pointed with his hand, 'Look, Pete, can you see that pile of stones down there and then, beyond them, where the hill shows against the sky, there is a bit of a dip?'

Pete followed his indicating fingers but it didn't mean anything to him. 'Eh? What do you mean? How is that going to help us?'

'Well, my friend Diana told me that ancient people marked things in straight lines, like standing stones, circles, mounds and things. She showed me them on a map, one behind the other. These rows seem to point to a circle or a village hut or something important. If you look around in all the other directions there is nothing, just more and more moor. That way I bet leads to the village hut circles and so to the others and old Larky. He will be pretty mad by now, I bet.'

'Dunno what you mean,' said Pete, looking very puzzled, 'You mean these old Bronze people set up lines of things, stones and such, to point to their villages. Are you sure?' he examined the distant hills but they were empty, still and silent in the small wind.

Paul assured him he knew what it was about and after a bit Susan, who had said nothing but shivered and clung to them, begged in a small voice to go somewhere, anywhere, as she was freezing to death. Give it a try, at least they could come back to the tall stone if it was wrong because the pile of stones and the notch would line up backwards and maybe from the notch they could see the school bus or the rest of the party.

Paul gathered up the two bags, Susan had lost the plastic carrier she had brought her tea in somewhere in the bog, and the board with the question sheet was muddy and bent where she had knelt on it in her struggle to get free of the clinging mud. Pete stuffed the board into his satchel and Paul slung his sports bag on its muddy but unbroken strap over his shoulder. He gently put his arm around Susan, feeling a fool but sure it was the right thing to do.

Carefully, Pete worked out the way, a straight line, past the edge of the dangerously green patch, still wearing its white fluffy tails of bog cotton grass, over the pile of stones. When they got there they could see that it was a deliberate heap not just broken granite chips caused by wind and weather. That gave them hope and they trudged up the next slope, keeping the rock pile lined up with the standing stone so that they didn't miss the dip in the ridge top. When they got there it was not obvious but in the distance, on the next ridge of hills, was another standing stone, shorter and fatter than the other, leaning a bit to the left but surely not a natural boulder.

In the valley between was a stream of water which Pete advised them not to drink from as sheep and animals might have caused it to be infected but they could wash their hands and faces. It made them feel a bit better. Where they came to the stream it seemed to have been widened out, so that animals could get down to the water and it shone, a small pool silvery against the green. It also lined up with the standing stone and the dip behind them. When they reached the squat stone they were delighted to see that the rough tumbled stones of Great Dog Tor showed clearly on the skyline and in the distance, a white speck against the dark tarmac parking place, the school minibus shone like a gem in a choppy sea.

Susan saw it and burst into tears again with some relief. She set off towards the bus with Paul and Pete close at her heels and as they ran to the safety and warmth of the familiar vehicle Paul could only think how grateful he was to the ancient people who had lined up those stones and mounds and pools so long ago.

Chapter Eight
A Losing and a Finding

A rather startled looking Mr Larkin listened as all three, talking at once, tried to explain what had happened, how they had managed to get covered with mud and why Susan, clad in too many clothes, was clearly very upset, with long pale streaks of tears down her very grubby face. Gradually he understood they had got lost and Susan had stumbled into a bog and eventually been rescued by the boys, although they were still lost in the mist which muffled the moor. Ignoring further details of their story he fetched cups of hot tea from the thermos in the van and offered them pieces of cake. Soon all three were feeling better and Susan, though still very muddy and unhappy, had begun to act normally. She striped off Paul's cagoule and Pete's jumper and returned them to their owners, so at least her top half looked fairly tidy.

The other children kept asking Paul and Pete questions but both were still a bit shaken by the events and didn't want to talk. They did not have very long to discuss the adventure as Mr Larkin told them all to get back into the van.

'I think, under the circumstances, we had better take Susan straight home so that I can explain what happened to get her into that state, so I'm sure you will agree to the sense of that.'

There were a few grumbles but Larky was in charge and Paul, for one, would be quite glad to get home. Soon the van was trundling over the cattle grid at the edge of the open moor and after enquiring where Susan lived he drove them to one of the nearby villages. Stopping the bus outside a neat white house he took Susan by the hand and led her to her own door. They vanished round the back and it was quite a while before the front door opened and Larky and Susan's mother appeared in the doorway. 'Thank you for bringing Susan home and telling me what happened.' she said, 'I expect she will have learned a valuable lesson about the moor today. She will be at school tomorrow if she is all right. Thank you again.'

'Now you lot,' said Larky, starting up the bus, 'the next stop on this mystery tour will be Paul's house, then Pete's and then I will take you others back to school as you can get home your usual ways.'

'You don't need to bother about me.' said Paul, but it wasn't long before they arrived outside Rose Cottage. Mr Larkin looked at him as if trying to decide something then said 'Go on in, lad, you acted very sensibly today but I expect you have learned a nasty lesson about the moors. I will talk to you at school tomorrow. Good evening.'

Paul grabbed his muddy bag, waved at the others in the minibus and ran up the path to the back door.

By now his parents were home and seeing the bus outside his mother had gone to the door to meet him. 'Good heavens, Paul, what on earth have you been doing? I thought you were looking at old houses not digging a hole in the mud.'

'Oh, Mum, it's all right. I slipped in a marshy place in the moor. I was trying to help one of the girls who had got into a marsh. It's only dirt and it was a smashing day out.' Suddenly Paul smiled, 'Tell you what, I have proved something that Diana told me about the way the ancient people built their monuments in straight lines. After supper can I go and tell her?'

'No you can't, you will get into the bath and then there might be a bit of supper for you afterwards, then early bed. I expect you have been up to something or they wouldn't have brought you to the door in the bus. Now get upstairs, there is a blue bath towel on the hot rail and clean the bath afterwards, I don't want black scum all over the place.'

Paul couldn't think of an answer to his mother so climbed the stairs to turn on the bath. As he went into his own room to undress he began to feel really tired. All the excitement had gone and left him feeling worn out. Soon he was immersed in warm soapy water and though he heard the ding dong of the doorbell he didn't take any notice. Sleepily he washed the dark peaty stains from his arms and face, the bath water getting a dark, foamy ring around the edge. He was almost asleep when his Dad called him down to supper. He quickly dried himself, sloshed around the bath with the sponge to remove the worst of the scum and clambered into his pyjamas and dressing gown.

Downstairs his supper of eggs and chips steamed on a plate. As he shook a generous helping of tomato ketchup onto his plate his father asked him about the outing. Between mouthfuls of hot chips Paul told a version of the day, explaining about the ancient hut circles and the question paper. He avoided details of Susan's adventure in the bog and his part in her rescue, saying only that the girl in their party had gone into the mud and he and Pete had got her out. He left out the sudden low mist too, saying only that they had navigated back to the main party by the straight line of ancient markers, which Diana had told him about.

When his story was finished, along with the eggs and chips and a plate of stewed apple and cream was following them down, his father said he should be very careful on the moor and try not to get filthy again. His mother looked around from her washing up and chivvied him off to bed as soon as his plate was empty. He was very relieved that no-one was angry at him and neither of his parents had asked any awkward questions. Soon after he climbed into bed he was fast asleep but he dreamed of a dark mire which clung to his feet as he tried to run from something he dare not look back at. By the morning he had managed to get some peaceful sleep and the door bell woke him as his mother was preparing breakfast.

'Paul, you getting up yet?' his mother called, 'There is someone to see you down here when you're dressed.'

Paul scrambled into some clean clothes and ran down the stairs, not sure who it could be calling so early in the morning. As he entered the kitchen the mystery was solved – it was Diana looking very worried.

'Hello, Paul,' she said, 'I heard about your adventure on the moor yesterday when I looked in last night but you were in the bath...'

'Did you move the big rock then and find something?' Paul said, very excited, 'I thought you promised you would wait for me.'

'No, it's not that, I've lost Clover. We were walking out beyond the dreadful farm of Nigel Blytes' when he came up behind me with his shotgun. He accused her of scaring his chickens by barking and running round their pens. He wouldn't wait for any explanation or even for me to catch her and put her lead on and get off the footpath through the field. He put the gun to his shoulder and fired over her head. Clover took off like a rocket and I haven't seen her since. She rushed away from him and his gun, I expect she knew he only wanted a small excuse to shoot her, beastly man. Anyway, I yelled and called all the evening then went home in case she had gone that way. This morning I am letting all the village know in case she has hidden in someone's shed or garden. Anyway, I called in last night to ask if you had seen her which of course you haven't judging by what your father said about your trip. Perhaps you could ask around at school in case one of the children or teachers comes across her. Poor dog, she must be scared out of her wits to vanish off like this and not come home where she knows she will be safe. I must go so that I can ask Mr Butterwort to mention it to his customers today, and also the post office. See you later perhaps.

Your father told me about the straight line of stones. We can have another look at the maps if Clover has turned up by teatime.'

Diana bid them all a swift goodbye and set off on her round of enquiries. 'Come on Paul, eat your breakfast and get ready for school.' his mother urged, 'I know you're worried by the dog vanishing like that but you can't help look for her until this evening. By then I expect she will have turned up safe and sound.'

'But Mum…' started Paul. 'No buts, get off to school,' put in his father, 'you have an important message to take from Diana and if Clover is important to you the sooner you can tell the local children at school the sooner she will be found. Now get on and do as Diana has asked you.'

Paul could see the sense of his father's argument so set off with his books to school. As he walked he scanned every hedge and garden in case Clover could have accidentally got shut in behind a gate too high to jump or a hedge too thick to scramble through. He saw nothing and arrived at the school gates feeling very worried.

After register Mr Larkin called him to come and explain what had happened the previous day and so Paul and Pete, who had been brought back from his own classroom to the empty staff room, told the true story of how Susan, so intent on picking flowers, had got into the bog and how they had managed to get her out, frightened but not hurt. Paul also explained how they had used the old standing stones as sign posts to find the ancient village and then the minibus. It didn't sound anything as scary to retell the adventure as it had been when they were actually lost in the mist but Mr Larkin seemed to understand what it had felt like.

'Well,' he said, 'I hope you lads have learned something about the moor and that you won't ever get lost there again. There is someone here who wants to see you to say thank you.' He opened the door and Susan, once more calm and clean, came in holding two packages wrapped in coloured paper. She looked embarrassed and silently handed one parcel to each of the boys, biting her lip and watching to see the reaction. Pete took his, muttered 'Thanks.' and immediately tore off the paper to reveal a box of sweets. Paul unwrapped his parcel more slowly, wondering if it was sweets too but as the last turn of paper fell away he saw it was a book, "An Illustrated History of Dartmoor". Inside Susan had written "To Paul, many thanks.' and there were several large XXXs.

'Thank you Susan, I don't deserve anything but I'm glad you're ok now.'

'Thank you for the sweets, you didn't need to give me anything,' said Pete, quietly.

'My mother said I must thank you because if you hadn't acted as you did I might have been sucked into the bog completely. It was bad enough anyway. I won't go on the moor again if I can help it. I hope you like the book, Paul, it seemed a bit heavy going to me but father said if you are new to the district it might be of interest. Thanks to you both.' Without another word she turned and disappeared through the door as fast as she could.

'Run along you two and don't go eating all those sweets in class, Pete.' Larky dismissed the boys who went back to join their own classes.

Paul couldn't concentrate, he knew he would rather be combing the moors for Clover and kept being told off by his teacher for not attending.

'Sorry, Miss,' he would say, but after the 4th time Miss Carter asked if there was trouble at home. 'Not at home, Miss, but my friend's dog has vanished and I promised to tell everyone at school in case they see her and can take her home. It's Diana Dymond's dog, called Clover, and she was shot at by Nigel Blytes. Diana hasn't seen her since yesterday afternoon.'

There was a mutter around the classroom as children recounted other acts of cruelty or nastiness which had involved Blytes or his farm. Most of the children knew Diana and her black and white dog and for a few moments the maths lesson ceased to interest them.

'Look, Paul, we must get on with this work but in the break you could write a notice and put it on the board by the main entrance so that everyone coming or going will see it. Does that help?' Miss Carter said gently, knowing the boy would not concentrate on his school work until something had been done.

'Thank you, Miss, I will do that.' Paul felt a bit relieved and tried to do the problems she set them. Soon the bell went for the morning break and Paul opened his desk to find a sheet of paper to write his message on for the board. He was still rummaging when Miss Carter leaned over and gave him a sheet of white cardboard which had been saved for some school project. She also lent Paul a red felt pen which would write more clearly than his ballpoint pen. For a moment Paul thought and then wrote in big but slightly wonky letters "LOST – CLOVER, BLACK and WHITE DOG belonging to Diana Dymond, Rowans, Micklehampton. LAST SEEN NEAR NIGEL BLYTES FARM." Any information, please tell PAUL SPARROW, class G4. When he had written the message as well as he could he took the sign and found a space on the notice board to pin it. Taking a couple of drawing pins from the bottoms of notice about school dinner money and football matches with another school, he fastened his notice where everyone would see it.

After the break he had a geography lesson which was mainly about drawing maps to show crops and produce of various places. For homework they had to take the duplicated outline map and fill in rivers, towns and all the information they could take from the textbook. It was then lunchtime with bangers and mash and the school's version of mushy peas and cold pears and custard. Paul ate in silence hoping someone would come up to him and bring news of Clover but no-one came.

After lunch he took the book Susan had given him into the field but didn't really feel like reading. He flicked through the pictures, many were churches or stately homes in the area and here and there were photographs of standing stones or circles of hut remains from the moor. Suddenly he recognised the ones that he had visited only yesterday and realised that it felt like ages ago. Perhaps there was something about Diana's Michael Church which could help with her original important quest.

He was still going through the index when the bell rang for afternoon lessons and he had to face French verbs followed by a history lesson. Somehow he got through these as most of the time was spent reading or listening to the teacher trying to get the Devon accents or the local children to sound even faintly French. History was more maps, following the Roman roads in England from Londinium to Deva, with names like Glevum, Corstopitum, Eboracum and Calleva scattered about. Paul soon drifted off to thinking about Clover and wondering where she might be. The teacher droned on and he didn't hear a word, not even the task set for homework. When the bell for the end of school rang he leapt up, without waiting to be told he could go, and shot out of the class, grabbing his bag on the way. His teacher was so astonished she didn't even call to him but one of the others explained about Clover and as the teacher had seen the notice she was not going to make a fuss. The other children soon followed Paul's speedy exit, some glancing at his red poster as they passed, but few really took any notice of it.

Paul ran all the way home and arrived, panting, determined to drop his bag of books and rush over to Diana's as fast as he could to see if Clover had been found. On the table was a package wrapped in silver foil and a note from his mother. He snatched both and dropping his satchel into a corner, ran out again without changing out of his school trousers and blazer into the old jeans he normally wore when traipsing around the fields.

He jogged through the village to Rowans, nestling under its low thatched roof in its nest of green trees and bright flowers. He banged on the back door but no barks answered him, no footsteps pattered towards the door. His knock was answered only by silence. Sadly he sat down on the doorstep to examine his mother's note and the package in case there was any clue as to what had happened. She had written in her small scrawly writing "Dear Paul, here is some tea as you will probably be out hunting the missing dog. No news when I went off to work but I hope Clover turns up all right. Don't be later than 9 o'clock or no supper. Love Mum." Inside the silver foil were some thick cheese and pickle sandwiches and a chunk of fruit cake and an apple.

Paul felt let down and uncertain as to what to do. After a few moments of doubt he stood up and reached for the handle of Diana's back door. He twisted it and pushed the door open. On the table was a piece of paper with his name on it propped up against a bottle of apple juice. He unfolded the note and read "Dear Paul, written at 3.30pm, Thursday. Still no news, no-one has seen Clover and though I have walked along the path across Blytes field without him seeing me today there is no sign of Clover. I do hope she is safe somewhere but I just can't think where. All the village is kindly looking too but no-one has any clue at all. See you about 4.15pm when I have been down to the river. Diana." It was a surprisingly ordinary note from Diana but looking at the clock on the wall above the shelf over the Aga he had only a few minutes to wait. In the meantime Paul helped himself to the apple juice and ate one of his mother's cheese sandwiches. There was nothing he could do except wait for Diana.

Soon the door opened and Diana came in. She was alone and looked very tired and fed up. Whatever she had learned had not helped with her search and Clover was still missing. Without a word she moved the kettle onto the hotplate of the Aga and quickly made a cup of coffee. Paul offered her a sandwich which she at first refused then, changing her mind, took one of the thick, crusty slices of bread and cheese, oozing dark, tasty pickle. As soon as she tasted the food Diana realised how hungry she was, not having had time for anything to eat since lunch the day before.

'I've searched everywhere and asked all the people round here. Needless to say, Nigel Blytes is not helpful but I saw he had gone out in that old wreck of a car this afternoon so I risked a walk across the fields but not a trace. I called and whistled but nothing, I can't think what else to do.'

'I know you must be worried. Clover is a super dog and I am sure she will turn up all right. I don't get the feeling anything really dreadful has happened to her, do you?' Paul said, trying to show how he cared.

'No, you're right. I can't do anything at present. If we stay here we might get a message from someone with news. Shall we go out into the garden and have a look at the stone we uncovered recently?'

Paul had almost forgotten his discovery and how it seemed at the time an important new clue in Diana's quest for the Hallows. So much had happened to him but now, as there was nothing useful he could do to help find clover, he might as well see if there was anything he could do on the original quest.

Outside the garden looked green and pleasant in the afternoon sunshine but both of them knew it would feel happier once Clover was back again to play and race about on the smooth lawn. Among the vegetables and against the back wall of the garden Paul hoped it would be possible to find another part of the mystery which surrounded the Dymond family. Behind the mound of compost on which the marrows grew there was a clear space where a stone carved with the big D had been uncovered and Paul thought it might be the hiding place of the 'shining stone' which was for Diana. When they reached the stone Diana had already brought a trowel and began to scrape the tufts of grass and weeds which grew between and over the stones of the wall.

Above the carved stone there was another huge plain rock, smothered in grass and trailing weeds, but when cleared it showed no carving or any way in which it might be moved. To each side the rocks were large and obviously couldn't be moved without pulling down the whole wall. The only place where they might find something was at the bottom and on pulling out the greenery below the carved block Diana immediately discovered small, rounded stones, not a great slab as there was on the other sides. When the plants were cleared out of the way Diana saw that it would be possible to get the rocks out without pulling down the great stone above.

Carefully she chipped with the trowel to loosen the earth and pebbles which filled the cracks between the stones. Paul stooped beside her, taking the handfuls of weeds to the compost heap and shifting the smaller stones as Diana shifted them. Finally there was one squarish stone left below the carved block and with a scrabble and heave Diana pulled it out. It came free with a rattle of small stones and a shower of dust which formed a mound below the great carved rock at the foot of the high stone hedge. Reaching into the dark space Diana leaned forward until her face was close against the cold granite. Her finger tips just touched something cool and smooth but beyond her reach. Crawling backwards Diana stood up and surveyed the garden, looking for a tool with which she could reach into the hole and pull out whatever was concealed there. She saw the long handled hoe and crossed the lawn to fetch it. Back on her hands and knees Diana reached into the dark recess with the hoe and swept around under the wall.

Gently she pulled the wooden handle towards her and with a sparkle of light a ball of some dark, shining substance rolled into the sunlight. Both of them gasped at the sight of this sphere of glittering glass. Diana picked it up, finding it cold to the touch and quite heavy. It was about 4 inches across and almost black, a globe of amazing crystal. It certainly fitted the description of "a shining stone" as the old verse said.

'Oh, Paul, it is beautiful. I wonder who put it there. It is lovely and to think it might have lain there hidden for hundreds of years, untouched and unspoilt. If it hadn't been for you looking for my vegetable knife it would never have come to light.' Together they walked back into the house where Diana took a clean cloth from over the Aga and wrapped the sphere, polishing its smooth surface and holding it partly covered up to the light. Indoors it looked dark green and though it was shining like glass it seemed too heavy.

Paul, who had been so surprised at the sudden emergence of the globe that he hadn't found words to say, suddenly burst out 'It's a crystal ball, you can see into the future or find lost things by gazing into it. It might help you find Clover. Do you know how to use it?'

'No, I don't, but I expect Granny's old book will have some information. I always thought of crystal balls as being clear, like glass, not dark like this. You may be right though, so I will fetch the book and see if there are any ideas in it. Put the kettle on and we can have a cuppa whilst we see what can be learned.'

Paul refilled the kettle and shifted it onto the hottest plate on the Aga. He reached down two brightly coloured mugs and the jar of coffee then the dark brown sugar which Diana preferred to white. He measured the coffee and sugar into the mugs, filled them as soon as the kettle boiled and then fetched the milk from the fridge. Taking a mug in each hand Paul walked through into the long living room where Diana was leaning over the table. 'Bring me the cake tin will you, after all this exercise I am feeling very peckish. Granny's book has no index so I can't just look up crystal balls and their uses.' Paul returned to the kitchen and reached down the big cake tin covered with painted roses. He wrenched off the lid as he carried it to Diana.

Inside were a few flapjacks, two pieces of sponge cake covered with pink icing and a lot of crumbs. Not a very interesting selection he thought but Diana didn't seem to care. She took a piece of sponge and ate it without looking up from the huge pages of the old book. After a few more minutes of page turning Diana suddenly pointed to a heading halfway down a page. 'To scry with a crystal or in ink or water in a glass. This is an art ruled by the moon and can be used to see into the future or to discover what people, being at a distance, are doing. It is not an art easily learned, some can scry and others cannot, but like many another art, it may be learned with patience.

Take the scrying glass, globe or crystal, dark mirror or bowl of clear water in which it is hoped to see and place it in a dim lighted place where there are no shadows or bright lights to distract the eyes. Place a clean white cloth below the glass and if you have sweet herbs put them on a low fire to give a smoke of moon scents. These will clear the inner eye and make the picture more easy to descry. Watch the glass in a dreamy mood and do not force pictures to come into the glass. Be still and seek the answer to a question in your mind. If the time is right a dimness will come over the glass like pale smoke blowing. In a while this will start to spin and then clear to a dark place in which what is to be will gradually appear. Be patient, watch without feeling and what is to be will unfold before you. If the spirit of the art is with you in time, within one moon, shall you master this art. If you are not so blessed you will see only your own face, dimly as in a dark mirror.'

'Do you understand all that?' asked Paul, stumbling over some of the more old fashioned words in the crabby script. 'It seems a bit like the dream spell but that worked alright. What about burning moon herbs again, did you use them all in the pillows?'

'No, I have plenty left. I would think poppy, moonwort and wintergreen might burn all right and there is some special charcoal which will light and give a glow to burn the herbs on. I will find it and a dish of heatproof pottery so that it will be safe.' Diana began to rummage in a dark cupboard and soon produced a small dish on a stem, a bit like those in ice cream parlours, and a round silver packet of black discs of charcoal.

Diana also found a clean white table cloth and carried all these to the table, placing the dish on a mat and opening the pack of charcoal and putting one piece into the dish. Quickly she fetched jars of dried herbs and a small spoon which she placed to hand. Carefully she made a mound of wrinkled up table cloth and wedged the dark globe in it. Finding a box of matches from among the odds and ends over the fireplace she lit one and held the flame against the black ring of charcoal which fizzled a bit and then glowed dull red. Diana drew the dark curtains across the wide window and in the low light studied the dark crystal to see if there were any gleams of light to spoil its polished surface. Glancing again at the old book she checked what she needed to do. Telling Paul to sit opposite her with a pen and pad to write down anything she saw as she began to sprinkle pinches of the greyish dried herbs. A thick cloud of white smoke arose from the hot charcoal making them both cough and splutter but after a few minutes it cleared to a gentle waft of strange scented air that hovered below the ceiling. Diana concentrated on the dark sphere and tried to ignore everything else. It was very quiet. Paul stared too but the cloth hid the shiny ball from him. The smoke made his eyes water and he wanted a drink but didn't like to move or disturb Diana. For a long time nothing happened then Diana looked up.

'It's no use, I can't see anything except my own face, upside down. If I stare at the globe it makes my eyes water and instead of getting pictures there's just eyes looking back at me. What can I do?' she ended miserably.

'Don't give up yet,' said Paul, 'the book said it was something you have to learn. Why not have a bit of supper if you are hungry and try again later on. I expect you can do it, surely you wouldn't discover something as important as that stone and then find it won't work for you. Do keep on trying, I'm sure you will be able to see things and find Clover. I just know you can.' Paul didn't understand how he knew but he was certain that Clover was safe and that Diana would find her soon.

Diana looked sad but nodded at the obvious sense of Paul's words and leaving the ball and the herbs went into the kitchen and absent-mindedly searched in the fridge for something to eat. Finding some bacon and eggs she soon had the big pan sizzling on the Aga with a slab of bread and some tomatoes. She offered Paul a share but he knew his mother would provide supper later on. Looking at the clock he realised how late it was. In the dimly lit room with the crystal, evening had turned into night without their noticing. He realised he must go home and saying a few words to encourage Diana with her studies he asked her to let him know at home if there was anything to report. Reluctantly he set off along the dark lanes to his own cottage.

Chapter Nine

A Spell for a Fine Day

Paul walked home, briefly greeted his parents who could see from his downcast expression that clover hadn't yet been found and didn't ask questions. He ate his supper without noticing what it was and miserably went off to bed, hoping the next day would bring something to be cheerful about. He slept deeply and didn't recall his dreams. In the morning he was still thinking how he could help but nothing came to mind. He silently ate the cereal for breakfast and picking up his books he set off for school. At least it was Friday and over the weekend he could join in the hunt or do something to help Diana. He realised that he hadn't done his homework but hoped he could get it done before his next lesson. Today he didn't care and if he got into trouble he would have to put up with it.

Just as he reached the school gate he noticed a familiar blue van and leaning from the driver's seat was Diana. She was smiling in a waning sort of way and immediately on seeing Paul climbed out of the old vehicle.

'No real news,' she called to him, 'but I did begin to get some misty images of the poor old dog in that crystal. I am sure she is alive and all right but in a small, dark place. I kept on as you had suggested and sometime in the early hours of the morning pictures began to come, not clear like TV, but shifting and blurred like reflections in water. Anyway, I feel certain she is ok and that soon

I will find her. I felt, too, that I could send her a message not to give up and that we would get to her soon. After the pictures of Clover I saw a soldier in armour who pointed with his sword and said "On my line, in the place of the sword, that which you seek will be found." I think it is real good news for I think the soldier was St Michael. He does keep on turning up around here so I feel a lot happier. After school, if you can, come and join me and we will search the lines of Michaels silver web. See you later, so have a good day.'

Paul was still trying to think of something to say but Diana had already dived into the van and was starting up and driving off before he had collected his thoughts. As most of the other children had gone into school and he could hear the bell ringing he had no time to contemplate what he might do. Cheered up by Diana's words he faced the lessons and breaks with a bit more enthusiasm than he had yesterday. Some of the children who had seen his notice in the hall asked if there was any news and he had little to tell them except he was sure Clover was still safe and would be found soon. Most of the children, living in the country, kept pets and knew how bleak the world could feel if a loved animal was ill or lost. He could feel their sympathy and it helped him through the day.

He paid little attention to any of the lessons, reading the books slowly and speaking to the teachers only when asked. Luckily most of the morning was taken up with lessons which did not require him to think for himself. Lunch was fish, mash and peas followed by fruit tart with custard. After lunch Pete came up to him on the field and asked what was happening about Clover. Paul told him there was no definite news but that he would help Diana search both that evening and all over the weekend if necessary until he knew what had happened to the black and white dog which had somehow come to matter so much to him. Pete said that he had to help his Dad weed his vegetable plot on the Friday evening but if Paul liked he would spend Saturday joining the hunt if it was still going on. Paul was pleased to have this offer from one of the local lads who would certainly know hiding places and sheds in and around the village that Diana might have missed. Pete said he would call in at Rose Cottage about nine in the morning and see what news had come to light by then.

'Cheer up, Sparrow,' said Pete, slapping him on the shoulder, 'we often lose animals round here but they usually come home safe. It's the cars that do more harm and then the poor creature on the road is found too easily. If Blytes didn't shoot her and she hasn't been injured on the road she's probably hiding somewhere around the moor or village. See ya in the morning then.' he called, running back into school as the first bell of the afternoon rang.

Again he was lucky and most of the afternoon was taken up with drawing and painting in the art room. Finally the bell rang and he was able to go home and see what the evening offered for the return of Clover.

The sky which had been grey and overcast now lowered and drizzle was gusting across the lanes and fields around the school. The houses and cottages were wrapped in grey mist and as Paul set off at a trot to get home the drizzle turned to real rain. Dull rumbles of thunder grumbled over the hills and lightning blinked in the sky. Paul did not have his waterproof cagoule with him and soon the rain soaked through his blazer and the legs of his trousers. He was really glad to get home and by the time he opened the back door of Rose Cottage he was wet through.

On the table was a collection of packets, a tin of soft drink and yet another note from his mother. Before he even thought about examining the items on the table he pulled off his wet jacket and hung it on the hook behind the door and then wrenched off his soggy shoes and socks and chucked them into the corner by the cooker. With bare feet he ran up the stairs to his own room where he shed the rest of his wet clothes. Rummaging in the chest of drawers he found clean pants, socks, a tee-shirt of faded yellow with 'Keep Britain Tidy' in orange letters across the front and a pair of jeans which seemed to have shrunk since he last wore them. He quickly dressed and jogged down to the kitchen to see what there was to eat. Unfolding his mother's note he saw that Diana had called in to say there was no news and that he was welcome to visit her during the evening. The foil packets contained thick ham and tomato sandwiches and a piece of chocolate cake. There was also a cereal bar which Paul ate rather than carrying it away. Shoving the packets of sandwiches and cake and a couple of apples from the fruit bowl into his backpack he searched for his waterproof. Not finding it behind the back door nor in the hall cupboard he had to return upstairs to his room. He unearthed the cagoule in a corner of the wardrobe and as the evening with all its rain had turned chilly he found a jersey and stuffed that in the bag with the food. Downstairs he pulled the cagoule over his head and found his rubber boots in the hall. Prepared for any weather with his food parcel, he set out into the pouring rain to see how Diana was getting on and if her crystal ball had revealed any further details of her missing dog's whereabouts.

Sploshing through the puddles which had formed in the lanes and dodging the worst waterfalls which plunged from cottage roofs, escaping down pipes and drains, Paul jogged as fast as he could through the sodden evening. Raindrops cooled his face and tickled down the collar of his cagoule and the heavy boots slithered on the wet road and made it hard to go as fast as he would have liked. Finally he arrived at the porch and knocked. His arrival was still greeted with silence but it didn't feel quite so bleak. Almost at once, Diana pulled open the door and ushered him into the kitchen where she helped him out of his soggy cagoule and oozing wellies. Steaming slightly he stood with his back to the Aga as Diana put on the kettle for a hot drink.

'There is a bit of news,' she said, 'one of the people who go into the shop had mentioned to Mr Butterwort that they had seen a white dog running like mad across the top moor on the day poor Clover vanished. If you look at the map you can see it is about a mile from Bytes' rotten farm. She could have gone that way and somehow got lost or stuck in a mire or something...' Diana's voice trailed off and she bit her lip.

'Look,' said Paul, 'it does give us a chance to know where to start. As soon as this rain eases off we will go where you said she had been seen and then comb the moor. All the kids from school said they would come, well, some of them anyway, if you give them a yell in the morning. Pete and his brother and some of the girls all want to help. Do you want a sandwich? Mum has made enough for two and I'm always eating your food.'

Paul fetched the packets and they both went into the sitting room with its collections of books and artefacts and maps. Diana spread a large scale map of the moor on the table and between bites of ham sandwich and gulps of rather hot coffee they examined the squiggly tracks on the moor, the different colours showing the varying heights. Out in the direction where the man in the village had suggested he saw a white dog there were piled rocks marked on the map, small steep cliffs and crags. A cluster of rocky peaks called Loose Bed Tors seemed to form a line across the map to the north of the Blytes farm but there were no clear tracks or paths leading that way.

'This area seems to be rocks not bogs,' said Paul, hopefully, 'perhaps there are caves or something.'

Diana studied the map in silence but after a bit admitted that it was better than a marshy area both to find, because of the high rocks, and to search as it wasn't boggy. Apart from agreeing to meet as early as Paul could get away in the morning and hoping for a fine day there was not a lot they could do.

'Can you do anything about the weather?' asked Paul, 'I mean, witches and that were supposed to be able to raise storms or calm the sea. What about a fine, dry morning with no fog on the moor.

Have you got a spell for that?'

'I'll go and look in Granny's book, there might be something there to help,' Diana said over her shoulder as she entered her dim little room under the stairs. Soon she came back with the big tatty old book and began to thumb through the pages.

'"To cure warts... to make any horse obey you whether its master will or no... to bring relief of the ague and the shaking sickness... to calm weather and bring a fine day for harvest" that's what we need, even if we aren't going out to cut hay.

"Take a new piece of string, at least your hands span in length, take it out into the bad weather and then calling upon the Old Ones in the sky to cease make three knots and as you pull each tight call "cease, cease, cease" and keep the string about you on the day that is meant to be dry. When ye need rain, untie the knots, showing them to the sky and call for rain as you do so." There you are, the very thing. I've got some new string in the kitchen.'

Diana soon fetched the ball of white string and a pair of scissors and cut off two lengths, each about a hand span long. Giving one to Paul she said, 'I suppose you want a go too. If it works you will be able to rent yourself to the vicar and charge him for keeping it dry on annual fete day. Come outside into this rotten rain and we will see what can be done about it. Ready? Right, here we go.'

'What sort of knot am I supposed to tie?' asked Paul.

'Any sort will do I expect, I have never heard of an anti-rain knot,' Diana told him, holding her piece aloft with three neat half-hitches in it. 'Cease, cease, cease, let us have a bit of peace.' she chanted. Paul followed suit, tugging the knots into his bit of string and holding it over his head. The rain took no notice and dripped from a leaden sky, down his bare arms and made dark spots on his yellow shirt. Diana shook the rain from her face and dashed into the kitchen for a towel. At least she was looking a bit more cheerful now. 'How old was my hedge?' she asked Paul, unexpectedly, 'Did Larky explain how you find out?'

'Yes, for every species of shrub in a 30 yard stretch of hedge it is 100 years old. We found six or seven plants which counted and that makes it at least six hundred years old. When was the garden laid out I wonder? It must have been about 1300 to 1400 if the plant count is right. Do you know?' Diana sighed and told Paul more about her family and their home on the moor.

Gradually the evening slipped by and, knowing that unless Paul got some sleep he wouldn't be any use for the hunt in the morning, chivvied him into his cagoule and out into the still pouring rain.

'Perhaps it is the wrong sort of string,' he said, stuffing the knotted piece into his pocket, 'perhaps it only works in daylight or for grannies or people who are harvesting or...' his voice faded as he jogged off into the darkness, squelching and splashing all the way home. His Mum was standing by the cooker as he came into the warm kitchen and she soon reached into the oven to bring out a plate of supper for Paul. There was lasagne, green beans and a grilled tomato but as far as Paul was concerned he could have been eating newspaper. It didn't take him long to finish that or the pot of cherry yoghurt which was in front of him.

As he was eating he kept on seeing Clover playing in the garden or looking sad when she had been told off. He saw her gnawing the bone he had brought as his first offering, he saw her as he felt she must be, cold, lonely and hungry, trapped or shut in some dark space as Diana described. He felt that somehow it was a part of Diana's quest for the Hallows that she had to lose something of value to find something else which was a prize.

He remembered the map she had shown him with the web in shining lines where holy places were and where there was a dark, knotted area, seeming to centre on Blytes evil farm. Something had to be done to make that part of the pattern clean and bright and he was certain that Clover vanishing forever could not be a good thing. She was such a happy dog, so friendly and clever. She had to be found and the mystery of the web uncovered somehow.

He was still thinking along these lines when, after a brief good night to his parents who both seemed engrossed in a play on TV, he went up to bed. He called over the banisters to his mother to wake him early so he could get out onto the moor. In his room he sorted through his pockets to find things which might be useful but he didn't have a real compass and his penknife had only one blade and that was very blunt. He found the piece of knotted string and, as a gesture, held it up to the window where rain still streamed in glassy trickles on the pane.

'Go on,' he said to the blustery sky, 'stop raining for us, help us to find Clover tomorrow. You don't need to rain do you?' A rattle of raindrops on the glass was his only answer and the sky was black and thickly covered with clouds.

Putting the string beside his penknife he continued to look through his pockets and came across a smooth, white pebble which, for a moment, puzzled him, then it seemed to warm up and tingle and he remembered the Unicorn and the Land of Legend. Without knowing quite why he held the stone in his clapped hands and called upon the Unicorn to help his quest in the morning. He remembered something about King Arthur, that he too had a white dog, and that there was a questing beast in the tales of the knights.

He was soon in bed and sleepily thinking about how to search a huge area of moor when there were only a few people. He dreamed of misty hills, purple and green in the dawn light and paths of silver thread forming patterns and a mesh of healthy, homely feelings over the land and as the dark hours passed a great figure seemed to rise out of the land, green clad, riding a greenish horse, with a tall helmet crowned with mighty antlers. 'I am the Lord of the Green Lands, I am the Hunter over the Hills, I am the Keeper of the Hallows in times of darkness and I shall ride with my red eared hounds on the Day of Judgement. That which is hidden in my empty lands shall be shown to you and my secret places shall be filled with light. May your quest succeed.' He rode away, across the wide landscape, over moor and forest and up into the pale morning sky and the baying of his hounds echoed in the silence.

Across the sky Paul saw a flash of dark birds, swooping and cawing as they headed for their nests in the tall trees beyond the church. There seemed to be the sound of distant thunder or someone chopping down a tree but Paul suddenly realised that it was his mother knocking on his bedroom door saying it was seven o'clock and was he getting up.

Soon he had scrambled into his clothes, washed the bits that showed, more to wake himself up than to please his mother, and stuffing the various things he had chosen into his jeans pocket he was ready to go down to breakfast when it occurred to him how quiet it was. One glance out of the window revealed a pale, sunny morning with wisps of white cloud scudding over the hills which shone green and plum coloured in the daylight. 'It works,' he almost yelled, stuffing the knotted string into his pocket, 'the old spell book was right and we shall have a fine day for the harvest. I do hope we find Clover today.' His mother, hearing the commotion, called to ask if he was ok.

'I'm all right, I just thought of something. It looks like it'll be a nice day. What's for breakfast?'

He quickly ate his bowl of cornflakes, toast and marmalade and a mug of tea and was pleased to see his mother making sandwiches of cold meat and wrapping some cake for him to take. His father had just glanced in as he tucked into his food and then vanished into the garage for Paul heard the door slam in the wind. Soon he came back carrying a small khaki knapsack with lots of pockets and straps and a water bottle covered with canvas. 'You might find these useful if you are going on a commando raid or whatever it is,' he said as Paul reached out and took them gratefully. 'If you wet the canvas round the water bottle when you fill it it will evaporate and keep the water inside cool. Hang it outside the knapsack on this strap and sling the lot over your shoulder and it won't get in your way. I did learn that much in the army.'

'Got anything to put things I find on the moor in?' Paul asked his mother as he stuffed his packets of sandwiches and cake into the knapsack. 'Diana is always finding things to eat on the moor and there might be mushrooms or blackberries or something.' She found a square plastic box and fitted it into the sack and with a smile she added a couple of silver wrapped chocolate biscuits.

'Good luck,' she called as Paul set off for the door, 'if anyone calls I'll tell them where you are and I do hope that dog turns up.'

'You don't want me to come too, do you?' his Dad said, picking up the paper, 'I will be around if you think I can help but I ought to check the oil in the car first.'

'I'll let you know once I have seen Diana if there is going to be a mass search we will rope in the whole village. Thanks for the bag, see ya later.' With a wave, Paul was off out of the gate and jogging down the lane to Rowans with his knapsack nudging his back as he went.

Chapter Ten
The Green Knight's Cave

When Paul reached Rowans, the kitchen looked like the headquarters of an Amazon expedition. Diana had a big green rucksack and was putting packets of food, bottles of drink, maps, a very posh Swiss knife with 27 gadgets for opening bottles, cans, splicing rope and getting things out of horses' hooves, as well as several blades for cutting. Paul coveted that knife more than anything else Diana had ever shown him. She filled the bag with a waterproof jacket, a woolly jumper and a shiny plastic sheet which she explained was a space blanket and would do for a ground sheet if they sat on the still wet moor grass to eat, it was also very warm if the weather changed for the worse.

Diana said the forecast was fair with south-westerly winds but these often brought rain and they should be prepared. Once the rucksack was packed she fitted a small pick into special straps at the back, saying over her shoulder as she shrugged her way into the harness, 'I don't see us actually needing an ice axe, but you just can't tell. If we set off towards Loose Bed Tors and explore from there we might be lucky. I have a feeling things will be all right, I seemed to dream of seeing Clover again, and at least the rain cleared up as requested. I must admit, the magic we have tried do seem to have been successful, but perhaps it is beginners' luck!'

They were soon trudging away from the village, over a stile onto the wet springy turf of the moor, here, near the village, grazed by sheep and shaggy black or russet cattle which roamed freely across the moor. To begin with they followed a path, going steadily, over hill and dale, through groves of tall golden glowing gorse bushes, ragged clumps of bracken, changing from green through yellow to rusty brown all over the moor, and great hummocks of heather, some still purple with flowers, with dull green leaves like crosses all down the stems. Here and there the path was rocky and Paul envied Diana in her strong yet comfortable looking hiking boots instead of his own scuffed shoes with soles which were rather too smooth for the rough going. Soon the village was hidden by the curves of the hills though a faint trace of smoke lifted into the light blue sky.

The sun rose higher and it got warm, feeling muggy even though there was a wind blowing across the open hills. After a while Diana declared a break, and finding some dry rocks, flat enough to sit on they both unwrapped a sandwich, and took a swig of drink from their bottles. As his Dad had said, the water was still cool and pleasant in the wet bottle.

'I had a weird dream last night,' Paul said, munching a cold beef sandwich, 'There was this green bloke, I think he was the same as I saw in that Arthur myth, but he had antlers and talked about hunting with red eared dogs.'

'Hounds,' Diana exclaimed, 'He is the hunter, called by some Herne, or even Gabriel and it is his strange pack that ride through the sky, chasing evil away...'

'You mean the Yell Hounds, Pete from the village was talking about them, they are supposed to have red ears.' said Paul.

'Yes, they have lots of names,' Diana added, 'and a whole selection of tales, some to do with Pwyll, he was the Lord of the Underworld, and then Gabriel who is an archangel, like Michael, but he is concerned with healing and the end of the world, you know, when he blows his trumpet.'

After picking up the pieces of wrapping paper and shoving them back into their packs, they trudged on towards a range of jagged rocks which now loomed on the horizon. The going was more rocky and the paths they followed were less clear, sometimes they actually had to scramble over boulders or clamber up sloping slabs of rough greyish granite. At every pile they explored in case there were caves or small places where the dog could have got trapped, but as the sun reached its zenith, they had no definite discoveries. There had been one false trail when Paul had spotted something whitish among some rocks at the bottom of a cleft and after a hard scramble and slither down to it had only found the tattered fleece of a long defunct sheep which had fallen into the crack and died there. It had shaken them both, and when they had clambered back to the top of the rocks they declared a break.

By now they were quite close to the tumbled rocks and great shattered slabs which formed the Loose Bed Tors and it was hard to see how they matched the neat lines and clearly defined cliffs and slopes as they were shown on the map. Close to they looked like a small mountain carelessly knocked to pieces by a demonic demolition expert and left in rough heaps all across the sky line. Here and there rocks seemed to form the remains of old walls or fences of small fields, others stuck up like tall fingers, and Paul was just about to ask Diana if she thought they were natural or had been put up by stone age folk. Looking upwards to some particularly tall boulders Paul suddenly saw what looked like antlers. 'Look,' he yelled, grabbing Diana's arm and pulling her round to look high up to their right. 'Is it a stag or something?'

Diana saw where he was pointing and certainly it did look as if a stag was hiding behind a pile of granite slabs about a hundred yards away. Without a word they both ran as quietly and swiftly as the rock strewn slope would allow to peer over the top of the tor. The antlers seemed to end in a shaggy green hat. 'It's the Green Knight,' Paul whispered as they drew near, 'He is resting with his back to that big rock, just over the hill brow. I'm sure I saw him move.'

They crept closer and as they approached the antlers they discovered they were only the bare branches of a stunted tree which had been wedged upright among the rocks for some reason. 'What a pity, I was sure we had found him,' Paul sounded miserable but was instantly alert as Diana said 'Listen.' Faintly there was a whine or a very quiet woof.

'Clover,' Diana yelled, and the faint sound was repeated, seeming to come from the very rocks beneath their feet. Diana scrambled over the top of the pile, down beside the stunted branch where the green scrub gave way to rock and found, under the rubble of slithered rocks, a small black hole. Clawing at the stones around it she enlarged it a bit and shoved her hand into the gap. A cold nose touched her fingers and a damp tongue lapped her hand.

'Clover, Oh Clover,' she cried, tears streaming down her face, 'Oh Paul, she is alive and she recognises me. Good dog, we will get you out as soon as we can.'

Carefully Diana surveyed the area. It seemed that somehow a lot of loose rocks had tumbled over a natural cave, blocking most of the door and walling up her dog who had sought cover from the fear of the shotgun. Now Diana could see how carefully they would have to work to clear a way out so that Clover could be brought back into daylight. For a while they laboured, carefully shifting all the small rocks and loose soil, bits of heather and rubbish which had come down over the hole but underneath they found a large rock had slid, blocking the way in. Even Paul's slender figure could not worm its way into the narrow space and they knew it was not possible to heave out the big slab without help, or risking bringing down the roof of the cavern.

'Listen, Paul,' said Diana, sounding serious, 'I think she is all right but I daren't risk that big boulder falling on her, after all this time. Can you run back to the village and get a couple of the men to come with heavy bars and a jack or something. Ask any of the farmers to give us a hand. I will give the poor dog a drink if I can. Have you by any chance got a dish, I only brought a bottle and she won't manage that.'

Paul immediately dug into his pack and pulled out the square plastic container, tore off the lid and sloshed some of his plain cold water into it. By lying on her face among the stones Diana could reach into the crack where Clover was trapped and gently nudged the box into the space. Immediately a black muzzle and pink tongue plunged into the water and they could both hear the sound of lapping. Clover soon finished the inch or so of water provided and Diana gave her another lot, taking Paul's bottle from him.

'What about something to eat? She must be starving by now.' Paul asked.

'I won't give her anything until we have got her out because if she is injured she might need to go to the vet for treatment. If she has eaten something it might delay being able to give her an anaesthetic. Better go hungry for a little while longer and be safe. Give me the map and I will show you the quickest way back. If you head for the next high spot in that direction,' Diana pointed to another rocky tor in the distance, 'beyond that you ought to be able to see St Michael's Tower and the trees of the village. I reckon it is about 2 miles in a straight line. You can do it in an hour and be back with help. It's twenty past two now, so with luck you ought to be back by half past three. Think you can manage?' Don't take anything but jog as fast as you can. If you meet anyone tell him or her what has happened and they can come up here, or carry a message to Mr Lennard, the vet, so much the better. Don't waste time.'

Paul needed no more urging, but set off down the rough slope, jogging when he could and running or walking as the ground allowed. It was very warm and though the wind still thrummed in the bracken it was not cooling as Paul went as fast as he could. The sky was clouding over and the sun kept disappearing behind clouds and casting fleeting shadows on the distant moor land.

After what seemed like an age Paul reached the next ridge of rocky land and was desperately hoping that the village would show on the horizon, but the green-russet-grey of the moor seemed to go on forever.

Looking downwards Paul found he was at the top of a steep, rocky chasm and it was not clear how he was going to get down. As the bottom a narrow stream gurgled between smooth boulders and fell over small waterfalls towards a marshy area to the right at the foot of the valley. For a time Paul struggled down the cliff but found he reached a ledge too high to jump down from and was forced to waste time clambering up. Moving further towards the boggy area the main gully was joined by smaller narrower valleys and he could manage to get down those. In his mind he kept on saying 'Clover is all right, she is safe, Diana will be able to rescue her, if only I can reach help soon.'

He was so intent on his mixed thoughts of success and determination to bring help when he missed his footing, and half slithered half fell right to the bottom of the cleft. Everything swung round and blurred into a dark whirling mass. He felt the blood pounding in his head and he felt sick. Gradually he was aware that he was cold and wet, and on forcing his eyes to open he found that he was lying half in the stream at the bottom of the valley.

Feeling very dizzy and sick he managed to get out of the water and knelt with his head hanging down, gulping for breath and trying to sort out his whirling head. On all fours he stayed, trying to remember what he was doing, where he was going in such a rush, then he remembered Clover and Diana's need for help to set her free. Paul struggled to his feet but found his left ankle had been wrenched in the tumble and as he put his weight onto it the sky began to swim around him and the grass at the side of the stream came up and clouted him again.

Slowly he sat up, gently he felt his left ankle, it was puffy and very sore. From his pocket he took a big hanky which his mother had given him, and after dipping it into the cold water he tied it round his foot and ankle. He struggled along the stream a short distance until he found a rough stick jammed among stones at the edge. With a wrench he pulled it free, and carefully clambered to his feet, putting his weight mostly on his right foot.

As he stood up he realised that he didn't know exactly where he had come from, or in which direction his shortest route home must lay. He groaned, Diana was relying on him to bring some men and here he was, lost in the middle of the moor with an injured leg. He sat on a stone, trying to think of an answer, afraid that if he just sat and waited for rescue the cave might fall in and hurt Clover who had somehow managed to survive so long. Desperately he felt through his pockets to see if there might be a match with which he could light a fire and make a smoke signal, or a bit of silver paper to make a mirror to shine sunlight flashes around, but he found only the blunt penknife and the smooth white pebble.

His fingers felt its polished surface, and almost dreamily he remembered the Unicorn's words, 'If you spin it on the ground the pointed end will always point to home...' Carefully Paul selected a flat piece of rock, laid the pebble on it and gave it a twirl. For a moment it spun madly then stopped, pointing along the valley. He spun it again and almost immediately it stopped, its sharper end aimed like an arrow head along the valley. With no other encouragement Paul set off, half hopping, half limping along to the end of the stream. After a while he found a faint track, slightly more level, climbing the side of the valley about the marshy place which, after Susan's experience, he was very keen to avoid. The path climbed, worn fairly smooth by passing sheep or cattle, who here and there had left their trademarks.

Avoiding the worst of the droppings Paul plodded steadily upwards, twisting along the edge of the valley, and where the path was joined by other faint tracks and there was a choice he spun the stone again. Each time it stopped firmly, pointing in one direction, towards home and help. Magic was still guiding him, even though he knew the path he was now following had not been marked on Diana's map, not did it seem to be the way she had shown him before he set off.

His ankle ached and the rough stick bruised his hand but he kept going, chanting 'Clover's ok, she's safe if I can get help. Clover's ok, I must get home.' until it made a sort of dance out of his uneven steps. He had got so engrossed in his chant and keeping going with his injured leg over the rough path that he had no time to look around or watch the sun's light casting racing shadows of clouds across the green moor or notice shapes made by man and not nature make peaks above the skyline. It wasn't until he found he was actually on a well trodden path that he looked up and saw that he was actually not too far from the village and on the path, a few hundred yards away he saw a familiar figure. 'Pete,' he yelled, 'we've found Clover. She's trapped in a cave under some rocks and we need some help to shift them. Could your Dad help?'

'No, he's not home at the moment but George, my big brother is in the village with the Land Rover. I'll get him and what about your Dad?'

'Good idea, I can't run because of my leg, I fell and twisted my ankle but I'll have to show you where Clover is. Can George pick me up at home in a couple of minutes?'

'All right, I'll get George and see who else can come and be at Rose Cottage, isn't it? Pete said, already turning round to run back to the village.

The last few hundred yards to his home seemed as long as the whole journey and though he was bursting with the news his foot ached badly and various other bruises that he hadn't noticed earlier began to throb. He felt a bit dizzy too and a nasty thudding feeling was in his head if he stamped too hard with his good leg. His Mum was at the door as he half staggered, half fell through the kitchen door.

'Hello, Mum,' he gasped, feeling very strange, 'we found Clover, she's ok but needs to be dug out of a cave in some rocks. Can Dad come back with me to give a hand?'

'You're not going anywhere, my lad, not with that injured leg, and you as white as a sheet,' his mother fussed, 'Sit down and let me look at it.'

'Oh, Mum, I've got to show the others where to go, it isn't far, and they won't ever find the place without help. I can manage if you can wrap my ankle in a stretchy bandage, and let me have a drink of squash. I am just a bit tired. It has been an adventure, I suppose. Where's Dad?'

At that moment his father came in from the garage, covered with grease and not in the best of tempers.

'Hello, Paul, what happened to you? Any luck?'

'Yes, Dad, we found Clover but she's stuck in a cave and needs a strong hand to get her out. Diana stayed with her and I ran as fast as I could to get back to get help. I fell down a gully and wrenched my ankle but it isn't much.' He bit his lip as his mother eased off his shoe and sock and began to bathe the now bluish and swollen ankle with icy water. Making a pad of some cotton wool she soaked it and slapped the chilly dressing onto the sorest place. Soon she had bandaged the whole area with a wide elastic bandage and fastened the end with a safety pin.

'That feels much better,' said Paul, through clenched teeth. His mother sounded worried as she finished the bandage. 'This is supposed to ease bruises. You better see if you can walk, 'cos I'm not allowing you out if it really is hurt badly.' She helped him to stand and he gingerly put the bandaged foot forward. It still ached but the bandage held it firmly and he could put some weight on it, with care. Just then there was a bang at the door and Pete and an older, taller version of himself stuck their heads in round the door.

'Not intruding, are we?' asked Pete, 'but I heard some help was needed and George has got the Land Rover outside. If Paul can show me on this map where to go we will get up there with Mr Sparrow too, if you want to come. There are some long bars in the truck and a hefty jack if it is needed. And spades and goodness knows what. Us farming folk is prepared for anything.' George was standing behind him, grinning but not saying anything as his young brother carried on into the kitchen as if he lived there.

Pete handed Paul a grubby map of the moor. It was older than Diana's sparkling new one and on a larger scale. Faint tracks were shown that hadn't been marked on hers and once Paul got the hang of it he soon traced the area of Loose Bed Tors and pointed it out to George.

'I know that area, lost some sheep up there once, they got stuck in the snow one winter a few years back and were sheltering among the crags. There's all sorts of caves and crannies up there, no wonder the dog got trapped. I reckon we can drive round the back lane onto the moor over the cattle grid, see it's a mile or two round but we can pick up this old trail across the moor and I think the old truck will go up there, especially if it's fairly dry on the tops. See, we can get to this place on the other side of Loose Bed Tors and walk in over the ridge, see, only about half a mile or less. You say the dog's trapped on the far side, there?' George pointed with a stubby finger at the greyish shadows of the rocks as they were marked on the map.

'Come on then, who's for the skylark?' he called, nudging Pete, and they both went out through the door closely followed by Paul and his Dad. His mother stood by the door, her mouth open as if to say something, but she didn't have time to utter a word before they had all piled into the truck and were roaring off down the lane.

'Good machines these,' said George to Paul's Dad who was in

the front, 'Go anywhere on a bit of diesel, ideal on this rough old moor country.' Paul didn't hear his Dad's reply as his voice was drowned by the roar of the engine as the Land Rover was driven off the surface of the lane beyond the cattle grid, onto a rough track. There was a louder roar and a lurch as George engaged four-wheel drive to get over the rocky ground.

For what seemed like ages they rocked and roared over grass and rocks, through streams and down gullies. Not going fast and lurching horribly on the steeper bits, but it was much easier than walking, if very much noisier. Paul felt Diana would hear the sound of the roaring motor in the silence of the moorland afternoon but he knew that at least George was prepared to drive across rough ground to find a place as near to the crag as he could.

Suddenly George brought the Land Rover round in a steep turn, charged up a slope, thudded over some rocks and came to a stop, leaning sharply to one side, on a bit of hillside which looked far too rough and stony for any kind of vehicle. George and Paul's Dad jumped out of the front and George unfastened the door to the back of the land rover to let Pete and Paul get out. Paul limped to the front of the Land Rover and looked around him. The rocks seemed unfamiliar and none of the peaks seemed to fit his memory of the place where Diana and he had found Clover. He was still staring around, seeking some landmark which would point him to the place at the top of the tor when he saw a flight of black birds, squawking high in the sky.

As he watched, they took on the formation he had seen in his dream and flew low over the jagged peaks, vanishing behind a tall finger of rock. Paul examined it closely and there, jutting against the sky, was a branch shaped like an antler and almost as he was ready to direct the others to the spot a figure appeared on the rocks, waving a jacket.

As Pete and Paul and George and Paul's Dad made their way up the tumbled rocks they carried some of the heavy tools out of the back of the truck, a long metal bar with a sharpened end, a jack which looked big enough to raise a lorry, some planks of wood and a heavy hammer. Paul was carrying the plank as he could use it as a sort of walking stick and as he trailed behind the fitter men he could see how Diana was smiling. She ignored the others and rushed straight up to him, threw her arms around him 'Oh, Paul, you managed it. You are clever,' then noticing his bandaged foot, 'What have you done to your leg? You got home with an injured ankle and still found people who would bring you back in the Land Rover.'

Paul felt a lump rising in his throat, he hated praise and knew he had been so nearly ready to give up when he fell down the gully, but he was pleased that he had managed to get help as quickly as he could for the slower journey to the village had been offset by the ride back and two hours had hardly passed.

Diana noticed how he looked and began to tell him about Clover, how she was in a small cave, the roof of which allowed her to stand up and even walk a couple of steps, how there was a flattish rock with a dent where rain the previous night must have formed a pool that she could drink. Diana said she had managed to reach in and stroke the dog all over and apart from her coat feeling dirty and full of grit from the cave she seemed unhurt. Clover was delighted to have been found and was still obedient to words to sit or lie down so she would do as she was told as the men set about freeing her from the cave.

George, who was used to shifting fallen trees or even large boulders in the fields of his farm, decided that if a lump of wood was pushed into one corner of the cave a jack could be set underneath to raise the large sloping rock which sealed the entrance. Gradually they positioned the bar and the planks to the best effect and Diana commanded Clover to lie down at the back of the cave. Slowly Paul's Dad and George worked the jack into position and began to lever it up, taking the strain.

Pete and Paul helped by scraping the smaller stones away and passing pieces of wood or the metal bar to whoever needed it. Diana was sitting down a little way to one side, trying not to keep on urging the men to get on with it. Paul moved over to join her and to keep her occupied told of his adventure in getting home, how he had been lost and confused by his fall and had remembered the stone. He felt in his pocket and took it out to show Diana and as he did so he felt it tingle and almost seemed to vibrate in his palm. 'Hey, it feels alive,' he cried, 'it's sort of buzzing, feel.' He passed it to Diana who almost dropped it when she felt the strange sensation.

'Didn't the Unicorn tell you that it meant something?' she asked, passing it back to him.

'Yes,' Paul answered, thinking hard, 'He said it would point to home, that it would burn with heat if there was danger nearby and it would tingle if one of the Hallows was near. It is definitely tingling out of those choices so we must be near one of the Treasures. Look, what are they doing now?'

The men had lifted the stone and by placing one of the planks to make a slope had allowed Clover a place to scramble up. She shot like a bullet straight into Diana's lap as she sat on the grass nearby and smothered her mistress with licks and snuffles. They both looked so happy Paul couldn't watch for he found his eyes going misty and a weird feeling in his stomach, almost as bad as when he had winded himself in a fall. Clover was safe and free, that was all that mattered.

To keep out of the way of the reunion he limped over to the hole where his Dad and Pete's brother were standing, surveying the results of their work. On the slab which closed in the back of the cave from which they had rescued Clover there seemed to be a sort of groove carved into a circle, no, as Paul examined it more closely he saw it was a spiral.

'Hey, Dad, look at this, there is a spiral cut into that rock, can you see?' His father and George both drew close to where he was pointing and his father traced the curves with his finger, somewhat grimy and scratched from his digging. Diana, with Clover close at her heels, came to look too and exclaimed that it was like the carvings at New Grange, a well preserved burial mound in Ireland.

'Perhaps it is a barrow, there are some in these parts I believe,' said Paul's Dad, examining other rocks in the cave, 'what is the name of the place? Loose Rocks or something?'

'Loose Bed Tors,' Diana said, 'Loose Bed, Llews Bed, the bed or grave of Llew or Lugh, he was a sun god. Look!'

The evening sky had now cleared and as they watched the sun began to set over the distant hill a ray of reddish light fell right onto the carved stone lighting up the spiral as it cast shadows of the taller upright stones on either side. The setting sun shifted in its downward course and, for a moment, the bare branch of the tree which marked the spot was shadowed onto the smoother plane of the boulder, the antlers moved across the stone, the Green Knight seemed almost to have come home. Diana and Paul looked at each other.

'One of the Hallows is here, isn't it? Under that carved rock or nearby? My stone tells me it is near, see how it is tingling when I touch it to the carving.' Paul held out the white pebble and Diana felt the buzz of force as it touched the surface of the stone.

'Yes, I am sure there is something here. We must arrange for experts to come and look. If we aren't too late back to the village I will ask the vicar. He knows several archaeologists round here and they are the best people to tell about something which might be important. Can we all get into the Land Rover? I don't know how to thank you people but you have no idea how grateful I am that you came so quickly and knew just what to do. There was no way I could move that stone to free this soppy dog and it would have been terrible to leave her there any longer. Please come back to

Rowans for a glass of wine or something.'

Paul looked at his Dad, 'Alright, old son, I guess you have earned it, if your foot is up to it but I think we ought to tell your mother first in case she thinks you've got lost as well.'

They all piled into the truck, George slammed the back door on Paul, Pete, Diana and Clover who was still showing delight at human company. It must have been dreadful for her, shut in a dark cave with no clear hope of rescue. Now it was over and soon she would be home in her own basket. Pushing the rucksack and Paul's knapsack from one of the seats in the back Diana sat down with Clover on her lap and Pete and Paul grabbed for handholds as the engine roared and George drove off the moor back to the road. It seemed to take a long time to get back to the village and the bumpy going and chugging engine made talking impossible.

Eventually they reached the village and drew up outside Paul's home. His Dad got down from the cab after telling him that he would walk round to Rowans a bit later on to give him a hand. As they passed the church Diana saw the vicar going into the vestry door and she called to George to stop a moment. She jumped from the van and ran up the path after the vicar. Clover, of course, ran after her, not wishing to be left behind ever again. Mr Pomeroy was delighted to see Diana and her missing pet and agreed he would contact his archaeological friends about the barrow on the moor and let her know what they had to say. Diana invited him to come along later for a glass of his favourite elderflower wine. He agreed, once he had closed up the church after his own Michaelmas meditation. George drove on as soon as Diana and Clover were back in the Land Rover and soon parked in the drive where her own blue van stood.

Inviting George and Pete in for the first time and allowing Paul to show them round the ground floor she got Clover to get into her basket and began to fetch something for her to eat out of the fridge. A plate of meat and biscuits vanished in a flash and the sound of slurping of water from her dish soon followed, showing that she was still feeling deprived. As soon as Clover had finished her meal Diana took a brush from its hook in the hall and began to brush the grime and dust from her white and black coat. It took ages as Clover squirmed and wiggled with pleasure until she was smooth and shining, her black face looked like coal and her body was as white as a sheet of new snow and her tail wagged as if it was about to come off. She was grinning all over her black, doggy face and, though she looked a bit thin and her paws were worn where she had scrabbled at the rock, she was well and the vet was not needed.

Chapter 11

St Michael's Protection

Once Clover was fed and watered and now shining clean again Diana began to see how she could deal with her human visitors. George and Pete had returned to the kitchen and after washing the grime off at the sink after their labours of digging Clover out they sat by the table waiting to see what happened next. Diana took a couple of bottles of wine from a rack in a corner and, giving a corkscrew to George, requested him to open them. She got Paul to collect some glasses from the dresser and set them out on the table. Pete was given the task of cutting slices from a large fruit cake and Diana dived into her fridge to fetch out butter and three sorts of cheese. She had hardly done this when a knock at the door set Clover barking like mad. It was the front door which surprised both Clover and Diana who dashed into the hall to discover who was choosing such an unexpected entrance in the country. It turned out to be both Paul's Mum and Dad who had not yet got used to the country idea of coming in back doors which were seldom locked. His mother was carrying a plastic bag and his Dad had a cake tin held carefully level.

'I hope you don't mind us both coming but Mary thought you might like a cake to go with the wine you offered me. I see you were prepared but here is a cherry cake to add to the feast.'

'We've also brought a bone for that dog of yours if she wants it. I cooked a joint of beef for lunch today which Paul missed so I brought the bones for Clover. Is that all right?' Paul's Mum held out a huge beef bone still well covered with meat to Diana. Clover nudged her mistress's knees and then stood on her back paws, nose raised and tail wagging expectantly.

'You never give up, do you dog?' said Diana, stroking her smooth head, 'Here you are but don't go burying it under my carpets. On the mat!' she ordered Clover who took the offering gently and went to the doormat to sample it. She had hardly had a lick when there was a knock on the back door and the vicar came in carrying a bunch of flowers.

'Thought you might like these,' he said, offering the bunch to Diana, 'they came out of the vicarage garden and are rather a good colour don't you think?'

Diana took the bunch and saw they were Michaelmas daisies, deep purple and mauve with bright yellow centres. She quickly found a tall vase, filled it with water and clearing a space on the dresser, put them in a prominent place. Remembering she was supposed to be hostess at this unofficial party she began to introduce Paul's parents to the others whilst everyone got a glass and a plate and began to help themselves to bread and cheese and a glass of wine, either pale gold and slightly sparkling elderflower or deep red blackberry, made several years ago and perfect for the occasion. Diana had given Paul a glass of blackcurrant juice topped up with soda so that it looked like red wine. He was delighted at not being left out. Pete and George had found some cider and were sampling that. Paul's Mum was asking Pete how they had rescued Clover and George and the vicar seemed to be engaged in a chat about farming prospects and what sort of harvest they would be celebrating at Harvest Festival in a few weeks time.

Diana was very quiet but Paul knew how glad she was that Clover had been found safe and well. He was sitting on the edge of the table to take the weight off his foot and eating mild white Cheshire cheese with sweet pickle on a real doorstep of bread as his slicing was not very straight.

After a while Paul's parents made the first move to go home and asked Paul to come but he said he would be home soon when Diana took Clover out a bit later on. They set off home after thanking Diana for the wine and saying what a delightful cottage and how glad they were that Paul had helped her find the dog and so on. Diana invited them to come to tea one day and have a look at the garden which was looking very good then.

Soon Pete and George decided to go home and, again, Diana thanked them for their help and gave them a big bottle of the cider to take with them. The vicar was also about to go when he remembered that Diana had asked him to contact his archaeological friends about her barrow.

'I spoke to Professor Sharp from Bristol,' he said, 'and it happens he is bringing some students down to the moor next month so he promises to come and talk about your site. As it is too far out of the village to get damaged by vandals or treasure hunters I expect it can be left until he arrives. Did you discover how the dog came to have got shut into the pile of rocks?'

'I think she must have rushed into a narrow gap which acted like a lobster pot, narrowing so that she could squeeze in but not out again. Perhaps her rush brought down some stones or one of the bigger ones shifted as she touched it. I just don't know but it was very fortunate that Paul spotted the entrance.' Diana did not like to tell the vicar about her crystal gazing or the dreams but she knew he understood about strange happenings, he was that sort of vicar.

'By the way,' he said, 'you know that carving on the tower? I discovered something about it. I was going to show you but with losing Clover and so on I forgot until now. Do you know what he is pointing at?'

'No, I can't guess,' Diana replied, 'it is roughly eastward, I do know. What is it?'

'Well, it's a bit dark now but one day you must come up and look,' he said, 'I'm not going to spoil the secret. You would have to come early though.'

'Oh, what is it? asked Paul, who was getting really keen on all the puzzles and mysteries which his new found friends talked about.

'Can't we go and see now? It's only quarter to eight.'

'Well, I promised to take Clover for a short walk towards your cottage and we do have to pass the church...' Diana began and the vicar laughed 'You young people, never prepared to let anything wait, are you? Hot rock music, rushing about all the time, discos and goodness knows what. All right, but I doubt if you will be able to see anything much.'

It took no time at all to find Clover's lead, grab coats and switch off the light before they were following the vicar, still chuckling to himself, towards the squat granite tower of St Michael's in the Moor. Taking a huge key from his pocket the vicar unlocked the porch door and instead of going into the nave he opened a narrow door in the wall of the tower, switching on a light as he did so.

'Go carefully, those steps are a bit uneven,' he directed them upwards, following until they came into the chamber where the six fine bells hung. Up the side of this was another narrow ladder of a stair which the vicar climbed first. He opened the door at the top and a ray of light shone on the stone parapet of the top tower. Helping Diana through, closely followed by Clover and Paul, he closed the door behind them. It was dark but below them the lights from the village shone in squares of yellow or brighter colours where curtains shaded windows. Above them the sky was black but the clouds of the afternoon had been swept away by the restless moorland wind and the stars glittered like points of white fire in the moonless night. At the top of the small turret from which they had come the golden cockerel of the weather vane swung gently facing south west. Turning towards the east the vicar directed them to look at the horizon. For a while they could see nothing but the shadow of the dark land against the paler sky and suddenly, as if by magic, a pale rim appeared. Diana gasped and even the vicar coughed. They had all forgotten that tonight there was a full moon, rising after sunset, and the shimmering white disc rose as they watched. Its base was marked with a small black dent, a tiny finger of rock shaded part of the moon's white face.

'I believe that is actually one of the highest rocks on Loose Bed Tors, according to the map it is anyway,' he said, 'I noticed it at sunrise the other morning when the sun rose about there, misty pink and pearly.'

Diana was enthralled for as the moon's pale light shone at a low angle across the countryside there seemed to be a silver sheen as if some of the strands of the silver web she had seen in her dreams where moon paths lit up by this strange, glimmering light. Gradually the circle of the moon rose higher and the pattern vanished, the land showing purple dark against the midnight blue sky.

Paul was looking all round and saw a different coloured glare, low down and to the left of where the moon had risen.

'Hey, someone's got a big bonfire down there, look!' he pointed to the reddish glow, 'It's a bit early for November the fifth.'

The others stared where he was pointing and being dazzled by the moon's brighter light took a moment or two to see what he was indicating.

'Someone's house is on fire I would think.' said Mr Pomeroy, 'Who lives out that way, there's the Samules and Hollies Farm and then Blytes place. It most likely is Grimpen don't you think? We better phone the fire brigade in case no-one else has done so yet.'

Without another word he shot back through the door, down the steep steps and through the church door. Clover, who had patiently been waiting, rushed up to Diana, jumping up and licking her hand. The vicar ran for his house next to the church and Paul, Diana and Clover followed close behind. When they reached the vicarage Mrs Pomeroy let them in as the vicar was already on the phone to emergency services. The nearest fire station was about ten miles away so it was a while before they heard the wailing siren coming through the village. By then other people had seen the glow or been alerted by Mr Pomeroy who knew extra hands might be needed. Jumping into the back of the vicar's battered little old car, with Clover clutched in his arms, Paul could hardly wait to find out what was happening. Diana sat in front next to Mr Pomeroy who let in the clutch with a bang and the small car rocked out into the lane. The flashing blue lights of the fire engine could be seen over the hedges as they followed in its wake. Several other farm vans and the square shape of George's Land Rover rushed along the twisty lane as fast as possible.

By the time they arrived at Grimpen, the house was well alight, flames leapt from the windows, and part of the roof of the lonely farm was beginning to fall in. The single fire appliance wasn't going to be able to quell the flames although the hoses sent sharp fingers of water splashing through empty windows and arching fire over the roof. Men from the village were filling buckets and passing them in a chain from the muddy ditch at the edge of the yard to a fireman who threw water as well as he could over the smouldering timbers.

Paul and Diana stood to one side with Clover, lurking like a pale ghost at Diana's feet. 'I don't think we can do a lot about this that will be helpful. The house is not likely to be quenched by these people at this later stage. I wonder what happened to Nigel Blytes, hope he's not in there.'

'Serve him right,' muttered Paul under his breath, 'he did shoot at Clover and drove her off into the hills didn't he?'

'Anyway, I don't think there is a lot of point for us to stay here now. You ought to be in bed with that sort foot of yours, which does seem to have recovered remarkably well!' Diana said, looking around. A car was pulling out of the yard and she waved to the driver to stop. It was Mr Butterwort the grocer. 'Can you give us a lift back please?' Diana asked and Mr Butterwort opened the door so that Diana could let Paul and Clover get into the back.

'Glad to see your dog turned up then,' said the grocer, driving carefully towards the village, 'Don't look as if there will be much left of old Blytes farmhouse. Good thing he was off in Exeter so some of the lads was saying. He won't be pleased to come home to the ruins, not with a sore head from too much beer, neither. Still, lucky it was the empty house and not the hen houses, poor battery birds wouldn't stand a chance if it was them that caught fire.'

Paul was no longer listening as they drove back but clasping Clover's warm fur he didn't notice his eyes closing nor his head nodding against the side of the car. When it drew up outside Rose Cottage he was sharply awakened by the door being opened and Clover leaping off his lap. With scarcely a word to Diana or the grocer he stumbled up the path to his back door. His mother could see how tired he was and instead of offering food or drinks simply watched as he limped up the stairs to his room. Creeping up a few minutes later she could see Paul fast asleep with smears of black soot on his face and the smell of burnt timber hanging about his grubby clothes, chucked on the floor. Picking up his jersey she could see it was covered with white dog hairs too and that there was a tear in his jeans which she hadn't noticed when looking at his injured foot.

Chapter 12
Pathways

After a rather restless night when his dreams featured slippery paths and falling rock Paul was pleased to wake and find the day looked bright. He recalled the previous day's adventures although his ankle reminded him that scrambling around on rocky Tors could have painful consequences. After he had got home, and eaten a late supper of hot soup, there had been a knock on the door and Diana, with Clover at her heels, had come to the house to bring some of her magical salve to aid the bruised and swollen ankle. Although Paul's mother didn't entirely like the look of the green ointment Paul encouraged here to spread it on his swollen foot and wrap it again. After a night's rest Paul discovered that the bandage was much looser and that when he put his foot on the floor he could stand and walk without pain.

Paul's Mum remarked on his wonderful recovery as he walked into the kitchen seeking breakfast.

'I suppose you will be wanting to go out with the dog and Diana again today?' she queried, pouring him a cup of tea. 'There's some fresh toast or you could have cereal and bananas. You heroes need to keep your strength up.'

Paul sat down to eat but already he was thinking about the strange discoveries. Soon he was able to go out into the early sunshine, promising not to go far, just to see how Clover was doing. Even going steadily it didn't take long to reach the gate of Rowans. Diana was in her garden picking some flowers and saw him walking along the lane.

'Hello, Paul,' she called as she spotted him hurrying along, 'Coming for a walk before the rain comes?'

Paul looked at the clear sky, 'Doesn't look like rain to me,' he said, catching Diana up. Clover danced around his feet, bowing and woofing and trying to persuade him to play.

'It didn't say so on the weather forecast either but I have a feeling we are in for a storm. Look at the colour of the hills.' Diana replied, pointing at the distant horizon. The green and purple moors were misty and there were sinister shadows with the hint of dark clouds building up in the distance. Gusts of wind stirred the bushes beside the road and whirled twists of dust from the gutter. There was an odd feeling in the air.

As they walked down through the village, Diana feeling that Clover and Paul had probably had enough of the moor for the moment, the bells of St Michael's church were ringing and Mr Pomeroy, in his Sunday cassock, clutching his prayer book, hurried towards the church gate.

'Nice morning,' he called, 'are you coming to evensong? Hello Paul.' But he didn't stop or pause for an answer.

'He knows I don't often go to church,' Diana said quietly to Paul, 'but he doesn't seem to mind. Since I have been on my own here he often comes and chats about anything interesting in the wildlife line or brings recipes from his wife. You should see the spread she puts on for the Harvest Supper which won't be long now. Everyone goes to church for harvest festival, often the Morris men come from Exeter or Widecombe and dance and there is a procession of all the villagers, each carrying flowers, fruit, vegetables or cakes. These are all put in the Church near the altar and after Evensong there is a great feast. You will have to get your parents to come and bring some of the lovely roses from your cottage garden. I am saving a huge marrow as well as some flowers. Have to see what I can find for you to take, if you want to join in.'

They walked briskly on across the centre of the village, along a lane with a low hedge bounding a field of cattle. Diana pointed out the qualities which made a good dairy cow and Paul tried to understand what she was saying. A large red-brown cow regarded Paul with serious dark eyes and casually licked her nose, poking her pink tongue into her nostrils, and then lowered her head to the rich green grass. Soon they turned a corner to complete a circuit of lanes and Paul could see the dark clouds looming over the moors and the sun began to vanish behind scudding clouds. The wind was rising too. Even Clover was not too keen on running far, she kept close to Diana, sniffing at the gateposts with little interest. As they turned the last corner coming back into Rowans' lane the first big drops of rain began to splash down and in the distance the rumble of thunder could be heard.

A great flash of lightning lit up the sky and so Paul and Diana ran the last couple of hundred yards to her cottage with Clover bounding along beside them. Almost as soon as they were inside the rain began to pour down and the crashes of thunder almost seemed to shake the walls. The wind rattled the windows and blew great gusts of rain against the glass with the power of a hosepipe. Diana soon had the kettle on and fetched one of her never emptying cake tins from the shelf. Today there wasn't much in it except a few crumbly biscuits as the hunt for Clover had taken all her time and cooking and other such tasks had been forgotten. They soon had hot drinks and on going into the sitting room it was so dark that they had to turn the light on.

'If it keeps on like this,' said Diana, shoving a pile of maps and papers off the edge of the table and setting down her mug, 'I will have to start lighting fires again.'

'It's nice to have a real fire,' said Paul through a mouthful of biscuit, 'we only had radiators in Hoxton and here we have a solid fuel boiler with a small fire behind glass doors in the sitting room, not a proper open fire to make toast on,' said Paul sadly.

'I don't know, you can open the doors in the winter and then make toast and when the coal is well alight you will be able to see pictures in the fire. I used to do that when I was younger. Now I've tried this crystal gazing lark perhaps I will still see pictures. You lose the knack as you get older,' Diana added, smiling, 'Never mind, what shall we do now? No dog hunt today, no need to indulge in ancient magic. I suppose I had better read some of the books I have been sent and start writing the reviews…'

Paul looked disappointed and the prospect of having to amuse himself whilst Diana read a book was not much fun, or he could go home through the pouring rain and continued thunder and help his parents. That wasn't much fun either. Then he noticed a twinkle in Diana's eye. She was up to something he was certain so, deciding to play along he said, 'Suppose I better go home then, if you've got work to do,' getting to his feet from the depths of the end of the saggy sofa and trying to push Clover off her end.

'You haven't finished your coffee yet,' said Diana, without looking, 'can't waste it you know.'

'All right, but I think you are up to something. What are you really going to do?' Paul retorted, sinking back into the soft cushions and letting Clover lay her shiny black head on his lap.

'Well,' said Diana mysteriously, 'I don't really know but I thought we could look at what we have discovered so far in our quest for the Hallows and see if it gives any kind of clue as to where the rest might be. There is no saying that they are all on the moor, of course, they could be anywhere in Britain or the world, I suppose, if they were magicked away by Merlin so long ago. Let's see what we have to go on.'

Diana pulled out the map from the crumpled heap on the floor and spread it among the artefacts on the table, then she brought out a small box of dark wood. Opening the lid she showed Paul the lamp from the chimney and the dark sphere of glass from the bottom of the hedge. Taking a red felt tip pen she marked a small star on Rowans and then a cross on St Michael's church. She added a mark on Loose Bed Tor, the cave of the Green Knight where poor Clover had been trapped. Looking over her shoulder Paul pointed 'Hey, doesn't that make a kind of arrowhead? The church and Rowans are at the bottom and the cave at the top, the point. Does that mean anything?'

'I don't know, almost every shape means something,' Diana said, peering at the map, 'It could be an arrow or the point of a sword or a star, all kinds of things. When I saw the web shape it didn't have any clear pattern, just lines merging on the village. It could be about anything and three points, not in a straight line, don't help. The things we found don't really tie in with the traditional Hallows, either, come to that. Perhaps we are following a wild goose chase.'

'What about that old poem, isn't there anything in there to show what we are looking for? It does talk about a shining stone after all and you didn't expect to find a crystal ball did you? You thought it would be a diamond.' Paul jumped up, 'Where did you put the parchment?'

Diana rose to her feet and went to the bottom cupboard under one of the overflowing bookcases. 'It should be here,' she said in a muffled voice, groping in the darkness. There was a rustling of paper and a kind of small avalanche slid out at her feet. From it she picked the crumpled page of the parchment and with it the typed version of the poem which she gave to Paul. 'Look, we have the Hallow from the hearth, if that oil lamp counts, and the shining stone. We don't yet know what Clover found in that cave but it is beneath the land or it could be beneath the stars and skies. We haven't found anything in a river so far or a sea and it talks of Hallows, plural. Perhaps there are several in the same place, like the lamp and stone were both close to here. Anyway, they are really only things which are of interest to you, aren't they? Isn't there any kind of spell we could do to discover the rest of the hiding places, haven't you seen any of old Granny's magic for treasure hunting? I want to see the other Hallows. There must be a way...' Paul was getting worked up. The whole thing was strange and yet he had a burning longing to continue the quest, if necessary rushing out into the storm which still rattled the windows and sent bright lances of lightening across the rain dark hills.

'Look, Paul, this quest has been going on for years, my father spent ages trying to unravel just one clue and in a few days you have helped turn up two of the treasures. Be patient. I expect we could find some more when the weather is better, after all, there is still the barrow where Clover was. There could be a whole heap of ancient things there, especially if it is a burial mound which hasn't been disturbed. It could almost be an English Tutankhamun's tomb, couldn't it? And you discovered it, after all.'

Paul looked sullen, the excitement of the last two or three days beginning to tell on him. Idly he reached out and picked up the dark crystal. It was cool and heavy and as he turned it in his hands thinking glumly of the rotten weather, the unsolved mysterious clues and all the strange things which had happened. He sunk deeper in his thoughts and Diana, not wanting to disturb him, quietly got up and drew the curtains against the rushing wind and pattering rain. Making only a small rustle and scratch with a match she lit the pile of bright paper and pine cones in the grate and walked away to find some small logs and some peat to drive off the chill of the very autumnal day. When she came back she was about to ask Paul to put some of the logs on the fire but she saw how intently he was staring into her crystal. He spoke, quietly, and his voice sounded far away.

'I can see the mist of the moor,' he muttered, 'and there is an old man in a long coat coming towards me. He is walking with a long stick of peeled wood and he seems to be coming very close. He wants to talk but there seems to be something between us. He is brushing it aside.'

To Paul the old man was as clear as if he stood before him and when he had made the brushing aside gesture Paul could hear him clearly. His voice was deep and slow, that of an old man, yet in the dark eyes set in a tanned face, partly hidden in long white hare and beard, there was a bright twinkle. He was absolutely real and Paul could see his long fingered hands clenching the wood of his staff.

'Hello, young Sparrow,' he said, 'you seem to have got very involved in my quest. Now, don't upset yourself...' Paul was about to speak but the old man continued, 'You have done great work so far. You may not be able to see some of the treasures because you have not found them in the form you would expect. When they were hidden they were changed, they were bespelled so that only those worthy would find them at all. Do you think you are really worthy yet? Eh? Well, lads have always been hasty and no doubt even today there are things you want that you can't have. Let me explain. If you listen you might see that you have indeed found all the treasures but only in a version which is suitable to your own quest...'

Again, Paul was about to protest but the old man went on, 'Some of the Hallows are powers, skills, strengths rather than objects. When you were lost on the moor with the little girl who was so frightened you were under the sky, beside the spring, within a sea of mud. There you found the "Power that brings man ease", you might call it common sense, another might say courage... Oh, no, I know what I am talking about... you acted with great sense and calmness. When you were still lost you didn't panic, you used your head, thought of the wisdom from times past which had been given to you and you dared to accept it. You could have wandered about on the moors for ages but you applied knowledge. That is a very great power.' For a moment the old man paused, he was smiling and again his hand gestured for silence as Paul wanted to deny his words. 'When you had found the white dog you set off to bring aid, you tumbled and were lost and hurt. The sky would not answer and you had no star to guide you home but you used the Mighty Power which you might call "magic" because you don't yet have a technological name for it. You were able to trust the spinning stone and it brought you to safety with speed. How long would you have lain there, waiting for others to find you, if you didn't trust to the power to get on alone? You could still be there, lost, hurt and frightened, but you did not think about giving up. There will be many times in your life when you will need to call upon that gift. No-one told you to look for the dog, no-one made you run so far. Out of friendship you offered help freely then you didn't seek treasure but you found it. You have your own shining stone, too, for the Unicorn's gift is more valuable than you think.

It still has many tasks to perform and so have you, young man. Because you have begun this quest you will not end it yet. Maybe you never will, but you are willing to reawaken the Old Magic in the land and use sense which many people ignore. You have opened some valuable gates so that the power, the blessings of the Hallows can again flow into your own world. Don't try to seek too many answers, time will bring them to you. You can always call on me, too, young birdling, for I am a hawk also. People used to call me Merlin, farewell...'

The vision faded, the glass darkened to near black and there was a great roll of thunder overhead. Paul jumped at the crash in the heavens and Diana reached out as the glass sphere fell from his fingers.

'What happened there,' said Paul, in his ordinary voice, sounding startled, 'I thought there was someone else here telling me about the other Hallows, how they could be feelings and things... I don't really understand. Did you see him? It was Merlin.'

Diana shook her head, 'No, I think he was in the scrying glass.

You seem to have done better than I did, you took to it naturally. I heard what you were saying though, perhaps you were repeating his words out loud. It makes sense to me. Of course the Hallows can take a different form, they are magic after all and have been hidden a long time. I don't think your quest is ended yet. What about some lunch?'

'Hey, what time is it?' Paul queried, 'I thought we had only just had coffee.'

'It's nearly one o'clock,' Diana answered, looking at her watch.

'Crumbs, I better go, Mum said you were very welcome to come along too as she imagined you hadn't had time to shop while you were looking for Clover. Will you come? I know Dad wants to talk to you about the area.'

'Yes, all right, I haven't got much in except some salad and cheese in the fridge. Are you sure she will have enough? What about Clover? I can leave her in the van outside.'

'Oh, don't worry, Mum is always sending her bones, I'm sure she won't mind her coming into the kitchen. We've never had any pets because they both work and London wasn't a good place to let animals roam all day. Is it still raining? Paul was going towards the window and Clover, hearing her name, nudged his knees with her shiny nose and wagged her tail expectantly.

Looking out Paul could see the storm had passed and the grey sky was lit by narrow shafts of sunlight. He followed Diana into the kitchen where she collected Clover's collar and lead and her own battered anorak, jingling the keys of the van. On opening the door though she could see the rain had stopped and the wind had died down completely during the time that Paul had been communing with Merlin in the crystal. Putting the keys back in her pocket and calling Clover to heel they set off along the lane. There was a gap in the hedge and looking over the gate they could see the moors rolling green and misty grey in the distance still topped with dark slate coloured clouds. As they looked, a stray finger of sunlight poked through the overcast and a beam of silvery-white light caught the dull hills, lighting them up with gleams of light.

'Look, the Silver Web, the sun has set it on fire,' yelled Paul, pointing to the sparkles of sunlight reflected from wet rock and winding pathways. 'It hasn't gone away.'

Other titles from Thoth Publications

A MODERN MAGICIAN'S HANDBOOK
By Marian Green

This book presents the ancient arts of magic, ritual and practical occult arts as used by modern ceremonial magicians and witches in a way that everyone can master, bringing them into the Age of Aquarius. Drawing on over three decades of practical experience, Marian Green offers a simple approach to the various skills and techniques that are needed to turn an interest into a working knowledge of magic.

Each section offers explanations, guidance and practical exercises in meditation, inner journeying, preparation for ritual, the arts of divination and many more of today's esoteric practices. No student is too young or too old to benefit from the material set out for them in this book, and its simple language may help even experienced magicians and witches understand their arts in greater depth.

ISBN 1-870450-43-4

THE GRAIL SEEKER'S COMPANION
By John Matthews & Marian Green

There have been many books about the Grail, written from many differing standpoints. Some have been practical, some purely historical, others literary, but this is the first Grail book which sets out to help the esoterically inclined seeker through the maze of symbolism, character and myth which surrounds the central point of the Grail.

In today's frantic world when many people have their material needs met some still seek spiritual fulfilment. They are drawn to explore the old philosophies and traditions, particularly that of our Western Celtic Heritage. It is here they encounter the quest for the Holy Grail, that mysterious object which will bring hope and healing to all. Some have come to recognise that they dwell in a spiritual wasteland and now search that symbol of the grail which may be the only remedy. Here is the guide book for the modern seeker, explaining the history and pointing clearly towards the Aquarian grail of the future.

John Matthews and Marian Green have each been involved in the study of the mysteries of Britain and the Grail myth for over thirty-five years. In *The Grail Seekers Companion* they have provided a guidebook not just to places, but to people, stories and theories surrounding the Grail. A reference book of Grail-ology, including history, ritual, meditation, advice and instruction. In short, everything you are likely to need before you set out on the most important adventure of your life.

This is the only book that points the way to the Holy Grail Quest in the 21st. century.

ISBN 1 870450 49 2

WITCHFATHER

A Life of Gerald Gardner Vol1. Into the Witch Cult

A Life of Gerald Gardner Vol2. From Witch Cult to Wicca

By Philip Heselton

From the author of the highly acclaimed "Wiccan Roots", this is the first full-length biography of Gerald Brosseau Gardner (1884-1964) - a very personal tale of the man who single-handedly brought about the revival of witchcraft in England in the mid 20th Century.

One evening in 1939, as the hounds of war were being unleashed, he was initiated into the 'witch cult' by these people, who called themselves 'the Wica'. Gardner was overwhelmed by the experience and was determined that the 'witch cult' should survive.

This book chronicles his efforts over the remaining quarter century of his life to ensure not only that it survived but that it would become the significant player on the world religious stage that it now is – "the only religion that England has ever given the world", in the words of Ronald Hutton, Professor of History at the University of Bristol, who calls it "... a very fine book: humane, intelligent, compassionate, shrewd, and based upon a colossal amount of primary research".

eBooks

Vol.1: ISBN 978-1-870450-83-6

Vol.2. ISBN 978-1-870450-84-3

Soft covers:

Vol.1. ISBN 978-1-870450-80-5

Vol.2. ISBN 978-1-870450-79-9

THE HIDDEN VALUES OF THE GOLDEN DAWN
Volume One: **We call thee to the Gentle Light**
By Rick Falconer
Forward by Charles Chic Cicero and Sandra Tabatha Cicero

These volumes are indispensible for any with a genuine interest in the Golden Dawn. They are no beginner's guides, for you are no beginner. The Hidden Values of the Golden Dawn is a series of Psycho/Spiritual Magical treatise aiding transformation to a Higher Magical Awareness. The Adept, student, and all with an interest in the Golden Dawn will find aspects of themselves within these volumes. They each form experiential and insightful importance, revealing an alchemical infusion and a depth shaping magical undercurrents to ever take you deeper into your artful journey with a gradual potential of Divine perfection.

Written a little differently, they do not form a historical account, nor will you find contained within the nature of an academic discourse. They are a communication to you from within the System itself as direct magical and spiritual teaching. Written on many levels by the Spirit for the Spirit - your Spirit, that they will find you their equal as a companion if you will allow, by words brought forth to touch you directly upon a deeper awareness and banish the façade of your intellect by a continual invocation of understanding and truth as an enfoldment of personal insight and inspiration.

Rick Falconer is an Adept of the Golden Dawn System and a member of various Rosicrucian and Esoteric bodies. Living in England he is a lifelong student of more than thirty years involvement in Hermeticism, including Golden Dawn, Esoteric, Pagan, Theosophical, Psychical Research and Spiritualist Organisations. He began his magical and spiritual vocation at the age of 11 with three Middle England Spiritualist Mediums in the mid 1970's.

ISBN 978-1-870450-88-1 soft cover
ISBN 978-1-870450-89-8 eBook

PRACTICAL MAGIC AND THE WESTERN MYSTERY TRADITION
Unpublished Essays and Articles by W. E. Butler.

W. E. Butler, a devoted friend and colleague of the celebrated occultist Dion Fortune, was among those who helped build the Society of the Inner Light into the foremost Mystery School of its day. He then went on to found his own school, the Servants of the Light, which still continues under the guidance of Dolores Ashcroft-Nowicki, herself an occultist and author of note and the editor and compiler of this volume.

Practical Magic of the Western Mystery Tradition is a collection of previously unpublished articles, training papers, and lectures covering many aspects of practical magic in the context of western occultism that show W. E. Butler not only as a leading figure in the magical tradition of the West, but also as one of its greatest teachers.

Subjects covered include:

What makes an Occultist
Ritual Training
Inner Plane Contacts and Rays
The Witch Cult
Keys in Practical Magic
Telesmatic Images
Words of Power
An Explanation of Some Psychic Phenomena

ISBN 1-870450-32-9

SPIRITUALISM AND OCCULTISM

By Dion Fortune with commentary edited by Gareth Knight

As well as being an occultist of the first rank, Dion Fortune was an accomplished medium. Thus she is able to explain the methods, technicalities and practical problems of trance mediumship from first hand experience. She describes exactly what it feels like to go into trance and the different types of being one may meet with beyond the usual spirit guides.

For most of her life her mediumistic abilities were known only to her immediate circle until, in the war years, she responded to the call to try to make a united front of occultists and spiritualists against the forces of materialism in the post-war world. At this point she wrote various articles for the spiritualist press and appeared as a speaker on several spiritualist platforms

This book contains her original work *Spiritualism in the Light of Occult Science* with commentaries by Gareth Knight that quote extensively from now largely unobtainable material that she wrote on the subject during her life, including transcripts from her own trance work and rare articles from old magazines and journals.

This book represents the fourth collaborative work between the two, *An Introduction to Ritual Magic, The Curcuit of Force,* and *Principles of Hermetic Philosophy* being already published in this series.

ISBN 1 870450 38 8

DION FORTUNE AND THE INNER LIGHT

By Gareth Knight

At last – a comprehensive biography of Dion Fortune based upon the archives of the Society of the Inner Light. As a result much comes to light that has never before been revealed. This includes:

Her early experiments in trance mediumship with her Golden Dawn teacher Maiya Curtis-Webb and in Glastonbury with Frederick Bligh Bond, famous for his psychic investigations of Glastonbury Abbey.

The circumstances of her first contact with the Masters and reception of "The Cosmic Doctrine" The ambitious plans of the Master of Medicine and the projected esoteric clinic with her husband in the role of Dr. Taverner.

The inside story of the confrontation between the Christian Mystic Lodge of the Theosophical Society of which she was president, and Bishop Piggot of the Liberal Catholic church, over the Star in the East movement and Krishnamurti. Also her group's experience of the magical conflict with Moina MacGregor Mathers.

How she and her husband befriended the young Israel Regardie, were present at his initiation into the Hermes Temple of the Stella Matutina, and suffered a second ejection from the Golden Dawn on his subsequent falling out with it.

Her renewed and highly secret contact with her old Golden Dawn teacher Maiya Tranchell-Hayes and their development of the esoteric side of the Arthurian legends.

Her peculiar and hitherto unknown work in policing the occult jurisdiction of the Master for whom she worked which brought her into unlikely contact with occultists such as Aleister Crowley.

Nor does the remarkable story end with her physical death for, through the mediumship of Margaret Lumley Brown and others, continued contacts with Dion Fortune have been reported over subsequent years.

ISBN 1-870450-50-7

AN INTRODUCTION TO RITUAL MAGIC

By Dion Fortune & Gareth Knight

At the time this was something of a unique event in esoteric publishing - a new book by the legendary Dion Fortune. Especially with its teachings on the theory and practice of ritual or ceremonial magic, by one who, like the heroine of two of her other novels, was undoubtedly "a mistress of that art".

In this work Dion Fortune deals in successive chapters with Types of Mind Working; Mind Training; The Use of Ritual; Psychic Perception; Ritual Initiation; The Reality of the Subtle Planes; Focusing the Magic Mirror; Channelling the Forces; The Form of the Ceremony; and The Purpose of Magic - with appendices on Talisman Magic and Astral Forms.

Each chapter is supplemented and expanded by a companion chapter on the same subject by Gareth Knight. In Dion Fortune's day the conventions of occult secrecy prevented her from being too explicit on the practical details of magic, except in works of fiction. These veils of secrecy having now been drawn back, Gareth Knight has taken the opportunity to fill in much practical information that Dion Fortune might well have included had she been writing today.

In short, in this unique collaboration of two magical practitioners and teachers, we are presented with a valuable and up-to-date text on the practice of ritual or ceremonial magic "as it is". That is to say, as a practical, spiritual, and psychic discipline, far removed from the lurid superstition and speculation that are the hall mark of its treatment in sensational journalism and channels of popular entertainment.

ISBN 1-870450 31 0 Deluxe Hardback Limited edition
ISBN 1-870450 26 4 Soft cover edition

PRINCIPLES OF HERMETIC PHILOSOPHY

By Dion Fortune & Gareth Knight

Principles of Hermetic Philosophy was the last known work written by Dion Fortune. It appeared in her Monthly letters to members and associates of the Society of the Inner Light between November 1942 and March 1944.

Her intention in this work is summed up in her own words: "The observations in these pages are an attempt to gather together the fragments of a forgotten wisdom and explain and expand them in the light of personal observation."

She was uniquely equipped to make highly significant personal observations in these matters as one of the leading practical occultists of her time. What is more, in these later works she feels less constrained by traditions of occult secrecy and takes an altogether more practical approach than in her earlier, well known textbooks.

Gareth Knight takes the opportunity to amplify her explanations and practical exercises with a series of full page illustrations, and provides a commentary on her work

ISBN 1-870450-34-5

THE STORY OF DION FORTUNE
As told to Charles Fielding and Carr Collins.

Dion Fortune and Aleister Crowley stand as the twentieth century's most influential leaders of the Western Esoteric Tradition. They were very different in their backgrounds, scholarship and style.

But, for many, Dion Fortune is the chosen exemplar of the Tradition - with no drugs, no homosexuality and no kinks. This book tells of her formative years and of her development.

At the end, she remains a complex and enigmatic figure, who can only be understood in the light of the system she evolved and worked to great effect.

There can be no definitive "Story of Dion Fortune". This book must remain incompete and full of errors. However, readers may find themselves led into an experience of initiation as envisaged by this fearless and dedicated woman.

ISBN 1-870450-33-7

THE FORGOTTEN MAGE

The Magical Lectures of Colonel C.R.F. Seymour.
Edited by Dolores Ashcroft-Nowicki

Charles Seymour was a man of many talents and considerable occult skills. The friend and confidant of Dion Fortune, he worked with her and his magical partner, Christine Hartley, for many productive years.

As one of the Inner Circle of Dion Fortune's Socicty of the Inner Light, Seymour was a High Priest in every sense of the word, but he was also one of the finest teachers of the occult art to emerge this century.

In the past, little of Seymour's work has been widely available, but in this volume Dolores Ashcroft-Nowicki, Director of Studies of the Servants of the Light School of Occult Science, has gathered together a selection of the best of Seymour's work. His complex scholarship and broad background knowledge of the Pagan traditions shine through in articles which include: The Meaning of Initiation; Magic in the Ancient Mystery Religions; The Esoteric Aspect of Religion; Meditations for Temple Novices; The Old Gods; The Ancient Nature Worship and The Children of the Great Mother.

ISBN 1-870450-29-9

THE WESTERN MYSTERY TRADITION
By Christine Hartley

A reissue of a classic work, by a pupil of Dion Fortune, on the mythical and historical roots of Western occultism.

Christine Hartley's aim was to demonstrate that we in the West, far from being dependent upon Eastern esoteric teachings, possess a rich and potent mystery tradition of our own, evoked and defined in myth, legend, folklore and song, and embodied in the legacy of Druidic culture.

More importantly, she provides practical guidelines for modern students of the ancient mysteries, 'The Western Mystery Tradition,' in Christine Hartley's view, 'is the basis of the Western religious feeling, the foundation of our spiritual life, the matrix of our religious formulae, whither we are aware of it or not. To it we owe the life and force of our spiritual life.'

ISBN 1-870450-24-8